Junker Dreams

Poetry by Paul D. Dickinson

High Kick To The Head
Cars, Bars and Electric Guitars

Junker Dreams
An Automotive Memoir

Paul D. Dickinson

Hopewell Publications

JUNKER DREAMS: AN AUTOMOTIVE MEMOIR
Copyright © 2019 by Paul D. Dickinson

Published by
Hopewell Publications, LLC
PO Box 11,
Titusville, NJ 08560-0011
(609) 818-1049

info@HopePubs.com
www.HopePubs.com

International Standard Book Number: 9781933435534

Library of Congress Control Number: 2019936608

Cover photo by Paul D. Dickinson
Interior photos by David Thiel
Author photo by Sean Smuda

First Edition

Printed in the United States of America

Dedicated, in loving memory
To
Michael Dowling Prichard
1968-2008

———————————————

You can live in a car, but you can't drive a house.
-Cheech & Chong

Table of Contents

Introduction

I trust any person more if he can drive a stick. If he can't drive a stick, then what the hell kind of a charmed life has this guy lived that he hasn't had to educate himself on manual transmissions?

My first lesson on shifting came when I was twelve and my much older brother was too drunk to push the pedals and shift at the same time. I did the pushing of the pedals and the steering wheel part, and he worked the shifter, selecting a close enough gear. I was terrified, but my brother needed cigarettes. We had to go.

I've never been well-off. Not that I'm opposed to it, but I am suspicious of it. Never have I owned a car I was afraid to abandon in a field, ditch, or junkyard if need should arise. There are a lot of people like me: Paul Dickinson, the author, being one. We have a bond through our car stories. I have broken down both on the busiest and the most remote roads in the U.S. and Canada, and I do not regret it. I wanted to write a book about all the times my various cars have given out leaving me stranded in many different locations. I wanted to title it "Breaking Down," and thought that it also might appeal to people with nervous disorders, increasing my market. I read Paul's book, *Junker Dreams*, however, and thought why bother with my book? Dickinson beat me to it. He lays out a much more enjoyable collection than this bitter manual shift driver could have ever done. Paul reminds us of the romance, tall tales, debt, camaraderie, adventure, and occasional solace that come with a junker.

Each car in *Junker Dreams* is its own character. Why can't we call all shitty cars just "Cars of character?" When a person buys a Car of Character, she is really buying into both a mystery and an adventure—a story she will be able to tell when she meets somebody who thinks he has it bad.

Junker Dreams

I have only once bought a car the "real" way through a dealership, and that's something I do regret. I was driving from northern Wisconsin down to Nashville, Tennessee, and my Escort Pony was making some funny noises. I knew it was time to bid adieu to that Car of Character before I'd have to spend money on another CV joint. It couldn't wait till Nashville. Driving through a small town somewhere in southern Wisconsin, I saw a different Ford Escort for sale, strategically parked at an appealing angle, it's nose dipping a little into the sidewalk space surrounding the Triangle Auto Sales lot. (Wow, I just realized I didn't even make it through one state before needing a new car.) It was similar to the car I was currently driving, yet way more expensive, so obviously it should have been a far better vehicle, right? THAT'S THE TRAP! Never fall for that. But I was desperate for a car that would get me to my job in Nashville at least on the right start day, if not the right start time.

I went through the car wash and then used the vacuum to clean up my old car, thinking a vacuumed car will fetch a much higher trade-in than a dirty car. Don't fall for that either: A car salesman cannot see clearly enough through his own dirty soul to notice the dirt inside your Ford Escort. It won't matter, so don't stop at the car wash.

I drove up into the lot and the old man pretended to negotiate with me. We made some small talk. He said, "You really shouldn't be so trusting of people out there in the world. Not everyone's like us," and then he sold me a piece of crap. I can't say he didn't warn me.

Five Ford Escorts have I purchased in my life, and only one gave me unreasonable amounts of trouble—the one that came from a legitimate dealer. A rip-off was way more likely to happen in southern Wisconsin versus northern Wisconsin, the more innocent half of the state. This southern Wisconsin car dealer was surely influenced by his proximity to Chicago where some of the shadiest deals in the world are made. I know it could have happened anywhere, but in defense of the state where I grew up, most people don't behave this unscrupulously in Wisconsin, so I blame it on Chicago. Indiana is geographically fortunate enough to do the same.

I grew up in the woods at least seven and a half hours north of Chicago. If you wanted something fixed, you usually had to do it yourself. "Fixed" for my family meant to make something tolerable. In high school, I'd borrow an old Escort wagon (the first in my series) from my mother to get to school. In order to get back home at night, I'd have to go out in front of the school, open the hood, and wedge my math pencil into the carburetor flap, jamming it open so air could get in and the car would start. The school secretaries watched me like I was stealing my own car, but it started and it was loud. It was not as loud as the yellow Vega with mismatched door my mom drove us around in elementary school. Once, we were pulled over at the grocery store by Barry the town cop for disturbing the peace. It's pretty hard to disturb the peace in a town where off-road mudding and shining for deer (preferably with a spot light attached to your truck's roll bar) were the popular after-school activities.

My dad was a mechanic, or that's what he said. Our family didn't own a set of Encyclopedia Britannica like a couple families in our town owned. You knew somebody's family was well-off if they even owned a partial set of encyclopedias. These were the same people that took their cars to town for magical things like repairs and tune-ups. What's a tune-up? That's what I wondered when I was little. Instead of displaying a partial set of encyclopedias, our bookshelf boasted a complete series of Chilton car repair guidebooks, the encyclopedia for cars. They were pine green, solid, hardcover books. They were the most noble, intelligent, and prized items in our house. When I was little, they were the ideal, heavy books to press four-leaf clovers between the pages.

Junker Dreams

Usually my pressings were interrupted by my dad who consulted these car encyclopedias even more than my mom consulted her Symptoms book, and that was a lot. When a man lives on dirt roads in the middle of nowhere, and has six kids who will all eventually purchase many cars for under four hundred dollars, the Chilton car books are more than just a manual. They are a survival guide, friendly companion, and worthy substitute for any Louis L'amour Western. Unfortunately, the cars kept getting newer, but the books never did. Computers entered the sacred car, and we were all at a loss. My dad was only good at fixing things up to a certain year, which was already way past the publication date of his Chilton collection. Computers wrecked everything, but not until after I learned about the basic inner workings of the car with my dad and siblings. It does give you a feeling of independence and pride to know you could change your own oil if you weren't too lazy.

I hadn't thought much about any of my car stories for a while, but all my own adventures, be they failures or successes, came back to me while reading Dickinson's work. When I laughed at Paul's stories, I laughed twice, having recalled a similar story of my own. One icy December day, I broke down on a bend where two major freeways merge in South Chicago. I was in an Escort, of course, and in rush hour, and in road construction. The freeway was a mess and I made it worse with my alternator dying on a nearly blind bend with only a couple feet of shoulder space. The temperature was five below zero, and I had no battery to run my heater or hazard lights for that matter, so I scrambled up the freeway embankment and through the construction like I was Lewis or Clark on a river expedition. I walked about half a mile through some higher numbered streets until seeing a McDonald's with an inexplicably large number of people standing outside it in the cold.

"Seems like the place to be," I thought. It looked like a political protest. After all, George W. Bush was in office. I got the tow truck dispatcher on my cell phone again and explained that although I had called him from the car before, I'd now be hanging out at that particular McDonald's on that particular street.

"I would advise you to go back to your vehicle, ma'am."

"But it's below zero, and I don't have any heat. There's people doing some sort of rally it looks like up ahead at the McDonald's."

"Those are crack addicts, ma'am. Please go back to your car."

I waited back in the car with my emergency blanket over me and wearing all my winter gear. It took an hour and a half for the tow truck driver to come and another hour for him to muster up the courage to pull my car out into speeding traffic on a low visibility curve. Apparently, this was the most dangerous situation he had encountered, and to combat it, he sent me walking down the freeway with a reflective vest and some orange flags to wave at oncoming cars, which only made the drivers stare at me instead of noticing my broken down car into which they came disconcertingly close to crashing.

That was the only tow truck driver (and I've had a lot) that ever cursed or showed any emotion at all. He did both openly in front of me and the rest of the drivers in Chicago that day. He swore more than Eddie Murphy swore on his first comedy album. I think this guy was born excitable and I don't think tow truck driver was his chosen profession. After a few months of operating tow truck in Chicago, I believe his nerves were frayed to where he was living one of Eddie Murphy's hyper characters, one of the crass ones before Eddie found God and Money.

Yes, this situation—life is a series of situations—was inconvenient, but I don't regret it. It gave me an excuse to not perform at that night's scheduled show in

Junker Dreams

Kentucky, a show I didn't want to do in the first place (and the only show I have ever missed, by the way). I do music and comedy shows for a living, so I drive a lot, sometimes unwillingly. I got out of that show honestly, and the Joliet, Illinois mechanics (smart of the driver to take me out of the city to get repairs) did a fine job on my fifth Ford Escort, the one my mother sold me. That car even made it out to California where I stored it under a friend's carport like one of Homer's sirens beckoning me to a life of gluttony where you don't have to shovel snow.

In *Junker Dreams*, Dickinson highlights the kinship among owners of Cars of Character. There is that for sure, but there is also an empathy I've gained through my car experiences, having relied many times on the kindness of strangers. I have empathy for anyone giving genuine effort yet still struggling, be it in their housing payments, employment, or other aspects of life. People in hard times help other people in hard times.

Readers will feel a connection to the culture behind *Junker Dreams*: A culture—or maybe social bracket is the word—of problem solving, thrifty creativity, ingenuity, and enjoyment of the moment's adventure. My rule for life has always been to do what you can with what you have, and help people because you know what it's like to need help. In one of my favorite stories in the book, Paul mentions the usefulness of bringing liquor to the negotiating table. So with that story in mind, I'm changing my credo to the following: Do what you can with what you have (yeah, yeah). Help people (uh huh). But remember it's okay to But remember it's okay to get what you want for REAL CHEAP as long as everybody had a good time. I like that scrappier, more junk yard style of thinking. It gives me some levity in my chaos. Thanks, Paul.

-Mary Mack

1997 Chevy Astro Van

Having my crappy slacker job and slowly going nowhere, in between girlfriends, manic episodes and any pressing engagements, I jumped at the opportunity to be a roadie for a rock band doing a Southern tour. I had been all over the South with my band and it was always a fascinating, if not dangerous, undertaking. In an attempt to be discrete , A brand-new Astro Van was cleverly rented by the band for this adventure. We wanted to appear like we were a family going to Disneyland.

When in New Orleans, it's important to go with the flow. If you think you're not going to drink, you will be crushed like a twig in a hurricane. The band played three gigs in New Orleans. I took my job very seriously, moving equipment and getting drinks for the band. Rock 'n' Roll is the best way to interact with the locals—you just never know what's going to happen. The first day there, we stayed with some punk rockers in a real dump. They were generous enough, but I wasn't interested in eating any vegan slop, not when I could eat oysters.

That first night it was raining like hell and I was happy just to have a roof over my head. Coming from Minnesota, I'd been though some crazy blizzards and tornados, but I'd never seen any rain like this. So in the middle of this storm, while I'm just hiding in my sleeping bag and hoping this ramshackle shack doesn't blow away, there is some sort of crazed emergency I get dragged into. Annie, the guitarist and singer from the local band we were crashing with is bawling, "I need to pick up my friend in the Quarter, we have to go get her, you have to help me!"

Who can resist a damsel in distress? Especially when she looks like Betty Grable with tattoos? So we got in her damn 1985 Chevy Van, all black with stickers, a real cop magnet. Thank God she was willing to drive, I wasn't too eager to blast through a tropical downpour. The lights worked, the wipers worked, and we rolled down the road.

Mardi Gras had just started and all my Southern adventures before this point suddenly became as innocent as child's play. It doesn't matter that it's raining like hell, the streets are full of people, and it turns out, a little too full. Annie has stopped crying and appears to be paying attention to the road. We are listening to a soothing Storm Troopers of Death (S.O.D) tape, attempting to get to our destination, where suddenly there is a blur to the left and a loud thud. We just ran over a human being-ouch. Annie is mortified. When we pull over, we see what appears to be a wounded sorority chick and that she is still alive. It is perhaps her inebriation that saved her from the impact. She was just so damn relaxed, she walked in front of a moving vehicle.

The girl had highlights in her hair, jeans, flip-flops and a was wearing a rather nice looking top. Running people over and killing them is never really something you ever want to be a part of, unless you are escaping armed attackers. I've been run over a few times, with minor injuries. But this, a 105-pound woman that bounced off the van, was a really bad scene. Yet like Lazarus rising from the dead, this casual Southern Belle got right up and really didn't seem to be any worse for wear.

Just as I was exulting in the joy of not being a participant in a homicide, a squad car pulls onto the scene. My heart just sank. I saw myself in the New Orleans Central Lockup trying to find something to make a shiv out of to defend myself. Annie is really freaking out because she has some warrants out for her somewhere in Louisiana. I'm was hoping the computers were down. We had about 30 seconds before the cop was out of the door and upon us. I repeated a mantra a friend out East taught me that got us out of a few jams, "Annie, all of our positive energy has to be focused on walking away from this without handcuffs." A southern criminal incident didn't seem like the place for New Age bullshit, but it was all I had. But to all of our amazement, the cop was laid back. I had expected a shakedown, frisking, interrogation and other legal forms of harassment.

"What's going on here?" he simply asked.

"I-I ran her over!" Annie blurts out, ignoring my attempt to put us in a Zen-like trance.

The cop looked at the victim, who was just kind of walking in a circle, seemingly more upset about spilling her beverage than anything else. He shines his huge cop flashlight on her, doesn't even speak to her, or ask if she is okay.

"Well," he muses. "It looks like she is fucking walking to me. Let's move it along."

We are stunned. We just stood there, frozen. If this were Minneapolis, we would be in jail and on the 10 o'clock news. Dear God, did I love the Southland.

We did indeed find Annie's friend. I wasn't really on the prowl, but I didn't want to go back to the punker house. Tommy and I decided that "I'm from up-river" would be our pick-up line. Tommy instantly met a girl who called herself Anastasia

Plus. She was a dark-haired beauty with a blond friend who seemed wispy and quiet, but "less than hostile."

For some reason, I wasn't on the make. I was on vacation, but I was also on vacation from being me. I made no moves on the ladies. It was like I was from the United Nations.

So things did improve. Anastasia Plus invited us to her large and comfortable home in the Garden District, where I stayed for the rest of my visit. One night we left the city with Anastasia and her wispy friend. We went to dark and bizarre after-parties held in ancient houses with booze and wayward souls. I danced; I danced like I was possessed. I shook off years of repressed Minnesota bullshit; long, cruel winters and broken hearts. I purged them from me with sea-breeze cocktails, insane beats and my own demented gyrations. I was far from home, able to be just a random partier from out of town. I recommend dancing over all forms of medical and psychological therapies. I drank myself sober and I danced myself away from the edge of madness and despair in America's only city-state, the port of New Orleans.

After we hit two parties, we decided to hit one more and as we cruised the dysfunctional roads trying to find the next destination, we got lost. I wasn't concerned until I turned to the local girls and said, "Hey, how do we get out of here and back to New Orleans?" They looked dumbfounded.

"Well," Anastasia Plus drawled, "We are here in the backwater, we don't know anything about no back water." Hmmm….

It's about four in the morning and even the locals are clueless, so Tommy and I dug out the map, which was underneath the Jägermeister bottle, (it is legal to drink and drive in Louisiana). I looked at him and he looked at me. I said the only thing that can be said and that is: "Japanese High Command." I slapped his face, he slapped mine. I slapped him again and he slapped me back. This cleared our heads and allowed us to make leadership decisions in a time of crisis.

We studied the map intently. Bit by bit, with Tommy at the wheel, full of caution and terror, and using only the map, not our brains, we worked our way back to New Orleans out of the medieval backwater in the sparkly red Astro Van. Anastasia Plus and her friend were asleep. I should have been passed out, but I was the copilot. I was awake, alive and ready for anything.

Volvo 242

1981 Volvo 242 Sedan

For a brief time in my life, I had the perfect car. I repainted my 1982 Volvo sedan. It was a two-door, which is pretty rare. It was a sophisticated dark grey color, actual BMW factory paint that a buddy of mine had "liberated" from his job at the body shop. I bought the car from the little sister of an old girlfriend, a classic bizarre St. Paul connection. All I knew was that it was a California car with no rust. I found receipts from a garage in San Francisco in the glove-box. This is the great thing about Volvos: They are bought and maintained, at least for a little while, by wealthy people. They still have that cachet, so a guy like me can become instantly middle class for $300.

I put in a brand-new Pirelli (an Italian company that contracts with various carmakers) interior from a junked white 1985 240 DL and this car was NICE! So I drove around in this fine machine, waiting for my life to become perfect. At the bar, I dropped the tale of my beautifully restored car into every conversation. I thought that all the ladies would flock to me. I thought, for the first time, I could actually pull my wheels right up in front of a place for a job interview, instead of parking down the block. The truth is that this wonder car had little effect upon my misery and desperation. As a two-bit mechanic, it was like building a fort when you were a kid; all the fun happened when you were done with the fort. This car was so mint that I was pulled over by the Minneapolis Police because they thought that the car was stolen. I was, after being searched, scrutinized and thankfully spared a beating, quite flattered by the incident. It proved that I had a car classier than myself. Who could ask for more?

Yet, as you might guess, my ride and I didn't have quite the Hollywood ending. Right in front of my house, as I was doing my 9 millionth U-turn on Selby Avenue, a St. Thomas girl in a Chevy Tahoe came out of nowhere and ran right into me. My beautiful carriage was trashed, bent in every direction. If I wasn't in that tank of a Volvo, I might not have survived. My only injury was a horrible insurance ruling against me, which seems as bad has having a felony for life on your record.

The funny thing is I actually had an amazing romance with a girl before I painted the car, when it was all dull and cracked. At least once in your life, you have to pick up a girl who works at a coffee shop. It's just a modern urban dynamic, a way of being thrust together by circumstance. She was from the local college and, as a life-long townie, I had certain aspirations. I started out by giving her foreign coins for tips. I don't know how or why I had these coins—French Francs, English Sterling, Italian Lire, Mexican Pesos. I had an active plan of seduction.

She was a natural beauty, a redhead, an actual California girl. She kept telling me about a boyfriend and I just changed the subject and kept talking nonstop. What is it about the moral relativism of Love? Sometimes you are the good guy, sometimes you are the bad guy. Sometimes you are the home-wrecker, sometimes you are getting your home wrecked. If you stick around long enough, you will indeed play all of the roles.

My little plan was slowly working. Then suddenly, an article in the St. Paul *Pioneer Press* appeared about me. It was about my gallery running the art tent at Lollapalooza. That day when I went to the coffee shop with my dwindling supply of foreign currency, she actually asked for my number. Later, after hours of staring at my ceiling, waiting for the phone to ring, it did. I was summoned to her upstairs duplex on Dayton Avenue that evening and suddenly I was the one being seduced. I stayed there until she had to go to the four pm shift at the coffee shop the next day. It was the beginning of a glorious summer together. High on life, I went out to get into my European sedan. For some reason, the Volvo wouldn't start. Dead. Not even a click. For once, I was OK, but the car was not. I remember just fooling around with it for a while, then just giving up and walking home. I felt like I really didn't need a car anymore. It turned out I was dead wrong.

Chevy Monte Carlo

1976 Chevrolet Monte Carlo

While the Volvo sedan was being restored, I drove around an uninsured, barely running, black Monte Carlo with plush red interior. It had very little heat and loved to kill at only the busiest of intersections. I, of course, am driving this beast through an unusually cruel winter even by Minnesota standards. Some people like to bungee jump or skydive. Some people like to go to Vegas or play the horses. I gambled with my life by driving an uninsured car with bald tires in rotten parts of town.

The "Monte" screamed sex, drugs and rock 'n' roll. It is the car of wild abandon with a menacing "Up Yours" sort of style. This is why the Monte is so beloved by every male member of the American population. Every time that car died I had all sorts of people rushing to my aid. All these blue-collar guys with huge trucks would stop in a heartbeat. They all had one, had the best times of their lives, perhaps lost their virginity at the 1978 senior prom in one of these cars.

At one point, I was driving in a blizzard on an ice-covered Highway 280 in the St. Paul/Lauderdale/Northeast Minneapolis triad of doom. I shouldn't have been on the road, I was just a plain fool. I've defied every travel ban known to the modern world: Hurricane, tornado, ice storm, locust storm. My policy was to just keep driving. I'm sure I thought I was going to score some priceless jazz records at the Goodwill while the entire terrified world stayed inside. Well, I spun out of control and ended up in the ditch, very stuck. Try as I might, I could not get it back on the road. At times of crisis, sometimes it is just best to be calm and wait for some sort of *Kung Fu* moment to arrive. I was sitting there in the freezing cold, sunk in my luxurious General Motors velour with a tiny dribble of heated air coming through the heat when a bunch of long-haired guys in a truck pulled in front of me.

"Do you need help?" yelled a guy with an Ozzy T-shirt and a leather jacket (it is true, there are people who wear a T-shirt and leather jacket whether it is 30 below or 98 above).

"Hell yes—and thank you!"

We hooked up a chain from his hitch to the front of the Monte and, after many attempts, got the damn thing back on the road. Just as I was thanking these dudes and insisting that they take a crumpled up $20 bill, a Minnesota State Trooper rolled up, lights flashing, blasting his siren.

"Oh, man," the heavy mental Good Samaritan groaned, "I'm not insured and my buddy has some warrants out…"

I shook his hand and finally succeed in pressing the money into his palm.

"Just get lost and keep moving," I told I him as I then turned around to deal with the Trooper. I wanted to distract him so he couldn't look up the plates on the truck. Luckily, he was in a real bad mood, too lazy to get out of his warm Crown Vic.

"Only licensed tow trucks can tow people."

"Well, sir, they just gave me a hand." I glanced down the road as I said this, happy in the fact that I barely see their tail lights. The icy wind was chilling me to the bone. He gave my car a sour, disgusted look.

"Looks like you were driving too goddamn fast."

"I'm just on my way home now, sir," was my frozen response. I was always polite with the police. Police are trained to ask the same question in many different ways to make you get defensive and start lying for no reason. I liked to limit those opportunities. I gently slid the Monte Carlo home. The blizzard continued and I laid low. I wrote a bunch of CD reviews and slept.

Do not underestimate the sentimental value men place on their vehicles. In fact, it is really hard to trust a guy who just doesn't give a damn about his wheels. It's like a mother who doesn't love her child. I've driven around in some real rust buckets in my time, a few that I curse aloud and even set on fire in bizarre ritualistic acts, but damn it if at the time, that car wasn't part of me and I wasn't part of that car. The lines really do blur between machine and man. This is the difference between gearheads and the rest of the world. We see the car's problems as our problems, not just as service or warranty issue. We can stand around for hours, drinking beer, just looking at an engine. The essential beauty and utility of a slightly outdated machine works strange wonders for the soul. Keeping the car going becomes an artistic and spiritual mission. It defies logic and common sense.

You really appreciate a car that works when you have driven so many that barely work at all. Perhaps I am guilty of being far too adaptable. That I can drive for months with no windshield wipers, or minimal brakes, or a passenger door, or rear window, or with a horn that starts honking on its own. You know you should fix it, but you don't get around to it. It is too hot or too cold, or it's almost payday, but then something else comes up and you just live with the problem for a little bit longer. You have fixed many problems before, so you know that it is just a matter of time. But that time just may run out and you have to pass all those problems along to someone else. This is what selling your car to someone else is all about.

Ford Escort

1985 Ford Escort (The Car Tape Loop)

Let me tell you about the 1985 Ford Escort GT. It was overheating, leaking oil and the clutch needed adjustment. You can never really trust the sticks on American cars, unless you have some super restored muscle car with a custom shift package. They don't have the advanced hydraulics of Honda and Toyota and a standard tranny is the exception, not the rule, in gringo cars. But I got this damn clutch set straight, replaced the valve cover gasket and threw in the little whirring fan that blows on the radiator. Now my product was ready for sale. My usual tactic was to go to the bar and discreetly ask people if they need a car. Or call every pretty girl I know, hoping I can be of some kind of assistance. And if I'm really desperate, I'd take out an ad in the paper. This can be a risky endeavor for it opens the floodgates for weirdoes that may call or show up at the door. Everyone from drug dealers, who might just decide to take the car right then and there, to arrogant Yuppies who just read some damn article in Consumer Digest or have seen an a televised special on used cars and have become instant experts. They are too important and professional to learn how a car works, but that doesn't stop them from bombarding you with useless questions that reveal their ignorance. My policy was to try and screen buyers out over the phone, try to find out if they are dangerous, useless or frivolous. Then I either had the car a few blocks from my abode or I meet them at a public place.

A Ford Escort is not a very exciting car. It had a little spoiler and decent power, but the name "Escort" is not very attractive. It is not a Volvo or a BMW or a classic car. It isn't even a thrifty Toyota that lasts forever. No, it's a damn Escort. It was, of course, uninsured and the license tabs had about a few weeks left. So, as usual, the car became my slave until I was able to sell it. It gave me a chance to give my regular machine a rest. Also, being quite paranoid, I find it helpful to change cars as often as possible to confuse concerned citizens and keep the ladies guessing. I had countless missions to run with the Escort: Picking up people at the airport, going to the bar, going to the scrapyard, looking for other half-dead vehicles, selling stuff found in dumpsters to pawn shops, and dragging my amp and guitar to gigs. Just the usual activities I engaged in while normal humans went to jobs, watched TV and ate balanced diets.

As I scurried about with my duties, I had plenty of time to enjoy the Escort's finest feature, a kickass tape deck. After a few tapes were shredded and thrown out the window, the tape unit settled down and I engaged in a profound sociological experiment: listening to a set selection of cassettes in a Zen-like frenzy. These weren't the mixed tapes that you make to impress a woman. These were tacky store-bough tapes that I found curbside after an eviction, (keep your eyes peeled on the 1st and the 15th).

My menu was a simple trinity: "Louder than Bombs" by the Smiths, "Kill Em All" by Metallica and "The Ramones" by the Ramones. I subjected myself to repeated, ruthless, and mechanical listening to this cacophony of rock. This was no random "mix" afforded by a multi-disc changer that could be found, say, in the trunk of a 1998 VW Golf. No way. It was one cassette, over and over until I went far beyond the breaking point, then put in the next tape and did the same, again and again. It brought me to another level of sanity via insanity. I was enveloped in a sea of endless repetition at high volume as I broke speed limits in every sector of Ramsey and Hennepin counties.

A new level of understanding washed over me. Morrissey, you whining Manchester wimp! I really wanted to hate you, but I couldn't do it! Because you were just so damn lost and forlorn; lonelier than Roy Orbison, almost as dreary as Ian Curtis. The fog of the moors came out of that cassette and covered road in front of me so that I could barely see. And Metallica, your guitars hurt my fillings, but I so enjoyed subjecting the entire world to your demented query via my crappy Ford factory speakers: "AM I EVIL? YES, I AM. "An aggression so pure that after the 16th time it put me at total peace. And the Ramones. What can I say about music that is so American, so PH-balanced to be in my bloodstream, so much an orchestra of the mind and body? That little tape had extensive life affirming nutrients. It could slay demons and seduce maidens. I think I almost melted it right into the tape deck.

I finally sold the car. It went to a good home. The buyer was an old co-worker of mine, He was so pleased he gave me a six-pack with the cash. It was a hot summer night in July in when he drove it away. I gave him a beer for the road. I left the cassettes in the car. They belonged to the red Escort and I didn't need them anymore. Those tunes are now implanted like a microchip, right behind my left ear. When I heard the familiar rumble of the exhaust, I leaned out of my window and watched the bright red taillights evaporate into the night.

Dodge Dart

1975 Dodge Dart

My brother and I shared this car. I think my mother traded an old oak table for it. He delivered pizzas in it at night and we both worked a bogus day job with it during the day. The job was call "Enumerating" for R.L. Polk and Company. They put out neighborhood phonebooks. We were making $3.35 an hour to walk door to door and ask nosy questions about everyone's family. Most people were just not home, or if they were home, they didn't want to give out information to a surly punk rocker. I think this job was left over from the 1950's.

We then discovered a new method. We would go to an apartment building and just write down all the names on the buzzer. This got our numbers way up. This went on for a few weeks. One day, we came into the office to pick up some more names. R.L. Polk was located on University Avenue, just on the Minneapolis side, in a fake colonial-style building. There was a huge lady with horn-rimmed glasses and a rubber thimble on her thumb. "Please, have a seat," she told us.

My brother and I sat down at a battered desk.

"We have some questions regarding the information you have been turning in."

There we were, getting $3.35 an hour, being interrogated like it was a national security issue. She placed the logbook on the table in front of us and paged through it with her gigantic hand and rubber thimble, which might have been for professional page-turning. "All these people you have listed as 'not at home'?" she asked us.

"They are all at work," we told her. "Nobody stays home anymore!" I thought this was a credible defense. She made a very large frown on her face.

"And this apartment building in Roseville, did you really talk to all these people?"

I was speechless. I had no response. I somehow telecommunicated with my brother. We got up.

"Um... we are done working here," I said. We got into the Dart and drove away.

The Dart had a few "issues." Like all Mopar products, there were bizarre electrical malfunctions that made no sense. It could have been "wire rot" or a ghost in the machine. The blinkers might work. Windshield wipers—a 50/50 chance. This was before I knew anything about fuses or connections, or really anything about cars, not that it would have helped. The worst problem was that the car would kill whenever you made a left-hand turn, which could get dangerous in busy intersections. We adapted and took as many right-hand turns as we could.

It is an understatement to say that women don't like being in a car when it breaks down. Once I was in the Dart on a date. For some reason, we were driving through the West Bank, a neighborhood in Minneapolis. Could I possible count all the flat tires I've had in my life? No. What was left of the tire was flapping around, smoking, so I had to pull over in a no-parking zone. There was nothing really left of the tire. I opened the trunk and found a half-inflated spare. Suddenly, every stumble-drunk yahoo wanted "help" as they eyed the girl nervously sitting in the passenger seat. I gripped the tire-iron nervously, but with conviction.

"No, I've got it under control, but thanks."

I was really a dork.

The jack provided by Mopar is, of course, some piece of shit bottle-jack. I followed the tire change protocol to the letter because I has already had a car fall off a jack.

Step 1: Loosen up all the lug nuts while the car is still on the ground.

Step 2: Jack up the car a bit and slide the dead tire underneath the front suspension, so you won't be crushed and your axle won't break if, says, some drunk bum on the West Bank decides to push your car off the jack.

Step 3: Take the lug nuts off the rest of the way, pull the bad tire off.

Step 4: Put the spare on the hub.

Step 5: Tighter the lug nuts most of the way.

Step 6: Pull the dead tire out from underneath the car.

Step: 7: Lower the jack and finish tightening the lug nuts with the tire-iron, as damn tight as you can possibly get them.

Step 8: Throw the dead tire in the trunk and drive away.

Before I could complete Step 8, a black dude approached me. "Hey, you got some pretty lame-looking tires." It was true. They were bald and the treads looked like paper towels.

"I can get you some brand-new tires for dirt cheap."

Hmm... I did like that "dirt cheap" part. His name was Joe and he gave me a piece of paper with his number on it.

A week later, my brother and I pulled into the parking lot of the Cedar Square Towers, a low-income high-rise on the West Bank. We waited. Just when I was about to give up, I saw Joe rolling, with considerable coordination and skill, four brand-new tires toward us. I had just finished my brief tenure at the downtown St. Paul Burger King and had cashed my one and only paycheck. I gave the man his $40 and put those beautiful tires in the Dart's trunk. But our transaction wasn't over yet, Joe needed a ride.

We followed directions to what I now realize was North Minneapolis. First, Joe had to stop at his "Auntie's" house. Man, he was in there for a long time. We were getting nervous. I considered taking off, but I really don't think we could have found our way back to St. Paul. Joe eventually reemerged. "OK, let's get your shit all mounted up and balanced. You know, my friends will do this for free, but it's a damn hot day."

I pulled into the liquor store parking lot and gave Joe $10. $50 for new tires mounted and balanced is still a great deal, right? The next stop was a garage, also in North Minneapolis. I couldn't find that place today to save my life. My brother and I sat on a bench in front of the shop while they drank the beer and mounted our tires. The entire procedure took about 45 minutes. Joe guided us back to the West Bank and we dropped him off. We never had a flat again in the Dart.

They say that tires are 90 percent of your ride, but our slick new tires from North Minneapolis couldn't really save the Dart. It started to leak transmission fluid profusely. We took it to a garage on Selby owned by a guy everyone called "Greasy Tony."

He said we needed a new transmission fluid pan. I got the car back, drove it for a few days and it leaked even worse. I brought it back to Greasy Tony. "Oh," he said after crawling underneath it. "I put the old pan back on instead of the new one." Hence began my longstanding suspicion of auto-repair garages.

Beside the toxic sludge leaking out of the transmission, which was sort of fixed by Greasy Tony, the car started to wobble in a strange way. So this time, I brought it to a garage down on West 7th. This guy was all doom and gloom.

"This car has a great engine. It will just rust around the engine."

I pictured the Dart disintegrating into nothingness, with me left sitting in the middle of the road, engine revving away. "Also, the hubs are so rusty that your wheels could fall off at any minute."

A little uneasy about having all of my tires fall off, we decided to sell the Dart, so that could be someone else's problem. I put my first "For Sale" sign in the window of a car. I forgot it was even there. We just kept driving the Dart fearlessly. Then one day, I was driving down Selby near Western and an old Buick Electra full of black guys pulled up alongside me, just about running me off the road. It seemed rather early in the day for a random racial incident.

I was a bit confused.

"The car!"

"What?"

"The damn car, how much for the car?"

I had completely forgotten that I had a sign in the window.

"Um, 150 dollars?" This was said with such lack of conviction that the dude just laughed.

"How about a 120?"

"Well... OK. Got the title?"

"Yep."

I had broken every rule by having the title in the glove-box. It was even all signed and ready to go.

"You know…" I stammered. "I was told the tires might fall off…"

"Really?"

"Yeah."

"Well, I guess I'll just take my chances."

I was surprised he didn't talk me down to an even hundred for my admission. I dated the title and grabbed some stuff out of the glove-box, then I handed over the title and he gave me the money. I walked home, hoping my brother would be happy with $60.

1986 Ford Escort

This was the only company car that I've ever used. And use it, I did. Those were the golden years of bohemia. I worked for the trendy Chinese restaurant. The Chinese owner didn't like the Japanese, so she had four gray Ford Escorts. I think the other drivers and I destroyed every single one of them. It wasn't out of malice or sabotage, but from being purely out of control and 22 years of age. I would ride my bike to work on Grand Avenue. I lived underneath the gallery. I paid no rent because the entire rent was paid for by our illicit rock shows. I would punch in on the register, get my giant cup full of Coke Classic and start booking rock shows. 4:30 p.m. was the best to reach rock musicians because it is the magic time between when they are asleep and drunk. Our delivery area was extensive. We delivered in both the best and worst areas of St. Paul. It was all the same to me because it was my town. We did Crocus Hill, Highland, Mac-Groveland, Selby-Dale, and Frogtown.

I liked delivering food. People were happy when you arrived. Every night was different. I had repeat customers. I brought beef lo mein to CEOs, hookers and drug dealers. And I kept this job, one step above fast-food slavery, for far too long because I was addicted to cash as well as the use of that zippy Escort. One person I got to know on the job was neither a hooker, a dealer, nor a CEO, it was the playwright August Wilson.

One night, I had my longest conversation with Mr. Wilson. I had some hyped-up theory about cultures coming in to collision. I didn't' really let on that most of it had to do with Wilson being half-German. He seemed to actually listen to me and tell me, probably to get rid of me, that "I might really be onto something…" Well, I left, high as a kite, thinking I was well on the way to being one of the great minds of my generation and I got into the grey Escort. Lost in my own mind, I turned off Holly and onto Dale Street and a blue Olds station wagon ran right into me. It crunched the front end of the Escort, making it completely immobile. I got ready to start yelling, when I saw that it was a woman with four small children. "Please," she said, "I don't have any insurance."

I told her to go. I walked down to the payphone on Grand Avenue. I called the manager and told him that the car was destroyed by a crazed hit-and-run. No, I didn't have a plate number. Yeah, I think it was a red car. I was fired and the glory days of a free car were over.

1969 Chevrolet Impala

Dear Lord, this was a car! It had the classic V8, 327 General Motors engine. I feel very sorry for people who have never driven a car with a V8, never felt the thunder of the insane beast, the crazy horsepower, the killer lurch of all the madmen that came before you. It was a faded green two-door, a damn land shark. It was jacked up, it didn't have a mag wheels. It was a sleeper. The Impala was a bit rusty, the exhaust leaked at toxic levels, but it could beat any other machine off the line. I bought it for $200 from a dude who installed and repaired washers and dryers for Sears. He had a great scam going where he took all the old units people were getting rid of, fixed them and sold them out of his garage. Another benefit of that gig was that you got to take the Sears van home with you and drive it like it was your personal vehicle. So, his Impala became available. But I'm talking so much about the car and machines and jobs and scams because, as a man, it is easier than talking about the woman.

And I did love her. H-Bomb and I, in our leather jackets, in my beat-to-shit Impala, we thought we were pretty cool. And I guess, in retrospect, we were. We were pretty damn "alternative." We lived illegally in a storefront. In the basement of the storefront we put on punk rock shows, also illegal. We worked our shit jobs at restaurants, but to us it was pure bohemia. It might have been Paris in the '20s as far as we were concerned. And I did love her, did I mention that?

I was, as Neil Young said, "lying in a burned-out basement" when I read my letter from the University of Massachusetts, telling me I had a fellowship and a stipend for their MFA program. I had never received an academic award, or even been on the Dean's List. I decided right then and there that I was going to go out East. I didn't ask H-Bomb, I told her. And I didn't ask her to come with me, I wanted her to stay behind and run the business.

Right after I received the letter from Donald Justice at UMass, the transmission from the Impala began to slip. It still had all of its gears going forward—even reverse, which is usually the first gear to go. What it lost was park. Park is a gear you don't notice because it keeps your car from going anywhere. The problem was when the Impala was parked, it moved up or down-hill. So my friend Mr. V made me some wooden wheel chocks just like the ones airplanes use. I drove that Impala for an entire summer, throwing those wheel chocks behind the rear wheel every time I parked the beast. The car was just for fun, fun, fun. It had an 8-ball on the shifter knob. It was a car designed for making out with a girl, with enough room in the backseat for a honeymoon suite.

Take my advice. Don't leave a car or a woman behind. When you come back, they won't be there. And although that Impala was pretty tough, a guy can always get another car. Women are much more complicated. And H-Bomb was a real woman, a woman who put up with a lot of my shit, my crazy ideas about the Art Gallery and my mad pursuit of poetry and rock 'n' roll. With that magic pale skin and cascading read hair, I knew she wouldn't wait very long. That she waited at all was a miracle. I am reminded of a solid fact: All of the problems in my life I created myself.

I came back that winter to the heartland and it was cold as hell. The space was thriving, H-Bomb, Mike and Mr. V had done a good job with the place. They had worked really hard. It was my turn, for the month of January, to get some shit done. I booked numerous rock shows and lined up some art. I had learned a few tricks from my numerous trips to SoHo. H-Bomb had finished off the transmission in the Impala and I had finished off my relationship with H-Bomb by being a calloused jerk and a lecherous fool. The emotional price I had to pay on that score would haunt me for years.

The Impala had become dead-weight in the gallery parking lot. The tabs were bad and the transmission was shot. It was piled up with snow, in the way of the plow. I dug it out. It fired right up! Damn, I had to say ciao to the beast. Mike helped me tow it over to the Central High School garage. There, Mr. Roth, the instructor, gave me $150 for the classic V8 engine, for his kids to study. He probably dropped it into some cool muscle car. Driving a car for more than a year for $50 was a pretty good deal. It was the last deal I was going to get for a very long time.

Buick Electra

1972 Buick Electra 225 Deuce

Mike had a black Buick Electra 225. The damn thing was massive. It was perhaps the largest car I have ever been in, a real boat. I really miss those huge cars. They were such a joy to drive, you felt invincible. You just wanted to cruise around, smoke cigarettes, call girls from payphones and buy strangers drinks at the bar. Under the hood, the Deuce had a 445 Rocket with a 4-barrel carburetor. We took it for granted and it just felt natural to have all that power. It was our right, it was the privilege of growing up in America to be able to step on the gas and fly through the night like a missile. With that crazed engine, a young man could have that special fantasy, the one where you outrun the State Patrol and fly across the North Dakota state line into freedom.

Yet, truth be told, we were not invincible in these glorious hunks of steel. Oh, no, there were the small people, those who lacked imagination and the ability to dream, they just couldn't leave a man and his machine in peace. And Mike wasn't about peace anyway, he was about chaos. Sometimes getting arrested is much like getting into an argument with a woman. One minute you are just driving down the road, the next minute everything just goes wrong. Now, I can't tell you exactly what happened to Mike regarding his encounter with St. Paul's finest. I can tell you that when he blasted out of the bat cave parking lot in the Deuce early that morning, he was sporting a spiked Mohawk hairstyle and wearing a leather jacket with no shirt.

But this I do know, I am always the guy people call from jail. I suppose I should take this as a compliment, but it does come with its challenges. What Mike had said to the cop at the Tobasi gas station on Selby and Milton must have been a stirring bit of oratory. It may have been regarding Mike's insurance, tabs, or driver's license, but I am sure to Mike it all boiled down to some grand repression of his freedom.

There was no way that I had the financial means to make the bail required, so I went to the bar where Mike worked. My thinking was *how were they going to deal with the oncoming weekend rush without their cook?* They knew me at the bar because twice a week Mr. V and I would mop the floors for cash, a free meal and a pitcher of beer. I'm not saying they liked me, but they knew me. The bar was still cool inside even though it must have been 80 degrees outside. It was sometime in the afternoon, but the place was rather full of daytime drinkers who looked at me with glazed eyes as the sunlight of the open door interrupted their tomb-like ritual.

Most bars have a creature known as the daytime barkeep. This specimen is typically old, male, cranky, Caucasian, and curt. He's not friendly, but he seems to be beloved by about three people in the world, usually drinking in silence at the bar, and that suits him just fine. As I strolled up to the bar, he gave me the "what-the-hell-do-you-want" look before I even opened my mouth.

So I skipped any cursory greeting and said, "Mike is in jail, I need bail money to get him out."

Then I told him the amount. The barkeep proceeded to unfurl an impressive string of obscenities that could have only been honed and perfected by a longtime member of his profession. He didn't ask why Mike was in jail. After his expletive rant, he became quite and just stared at me. I didn't know what to do, so I stared back. And everyone in the bar was staring at both of us. Then with great ceremony, he punched the No Sale button that opened that ancient cash register. This whole time he just stared at me with an acute sense of power, that he could make or break my little punk friends and me. But his actions were so controlled and automatic, I could tell this wasn't the first time the bar had rescued one of her own. And that bartender, a true jerk by any measure, nevertheless lived by code, a code that could be understood by those who drove a 1972 Buick Electra. This code, almost genetic at this point, told him that you don't leave a member of your crew in jail. Mr. Cranky Pants then pulled up the plastic cash drawer and handed me a wad of 100 dollar bills. "Tell Mike he better not be late."

Dodge Colt

1981 Brown Dodge Colt

By some miracle I was rehired a few years after destroying the Escort, at a different branch of the Chinese place. In their system, the manager was all-powerful and this guy was an old friend. Yet I wasn't able to start driving right away. I worked my way up to delivery, the king of slacker jobs. I was a prep cook, and then I became a stir-fry Samurai, which I actually really enjoyed.

So this car was purchased from a fellow fry cook at the Chinese place. I paid $110 for it. It was an amazing little delivery machine. These Colts had little Mitsubishi engines that ran forever. I was just doing my thing, the punk rock way, the underground way. Furniture to antique stores, electronics to pawnshops, scrap metal to the scrapyards—cash under the mattress.

I even got another job during the day. It is true, sometimes in my life I would just make some $$ and buy myself some time. I'd live off of it for a while and just ride my bicycle around, write poetry, and drink beer in people's garages. Not truly any sort of career path. Yet then I would have fits of multi-employment where I'd just work, work, work a collection of shitty jobs until I realized how stupid it all was.

I became a physical therapy assistant at an upscale nursing home in Como Park. I liked the old folks. The old men would be in some narcotic haze as I pushed them around in their wheelchairs. I'd lean over real close and say, "Hey, what was your favorite car?" and through the mists of memory, dementia and Lord knows what else, they always had a crystal clear answer for me, "39 Pontiac," "63 Lincoln,"

Junker Dreams

"52 Packard," so happy that someone finally asked them about something that actually mattered.

My schedule was this: 7am to 2pm at the nursing home, and then from 4pm to 10pm at the Chinese restaurant. I really needed to have that twenty-two minute power nap on my couch between shifts. Then one day, I agreed to go read poetry at the REV105 radio station. I got out of my evening shift, but there was not time for my nap. I drove directly to downtown Minneapolis from the nursing home; I think I was still wearing my stupid nametag. I was completely in my head, working out my poetry when I drove right through a red light in the middle of downtown Mill City.

A lady in a Nissan T-boned me. I spun around and hit the stoplight on the other side of the street. I was bleeding, my glasses broken. When the cops arrived I was trying to pry the front of my car off the light-pole with a crowbar, which didn't make them happy. The Nissan woman was checked out in an ambulance and released. They examined me, right after I saw them tow away the Colt. Hmm... It looked drivable to me. I found a payphone. I called the radio station, told them I couldn't make it, then called an ex-girlfriend, looking for some sympathy (didn't really work) and then I took a damn bus back to St. Paul.

Things were not looking good for me. 1) I lost my car and my ability to make cash money delivering food. 2) My insurance rates were about to soar. 3) My last known female companion couldn't elicit sympathy for me even after a bloody car crash. 4) I was charged with reckless driving in Hennepin County, which means I was facing jail time, fines and loss of license. I sat on that red city bus and thanked the Irish Catholic God of St. Paul that my sister's husband was a lawyer.

My advice to you is to never go into the Hennepin County Government Center for any reason. I went because my name was on a courtroom docket. My brother-in-law didn't represent me. He did corporate law, so he got a good friend of his, a criminal lawyer, to save my sorry ass. I knew I was wasting this guys time, and it made me feel even worse.

There I sat, packed on a bench with the rest of the criminals in the back of the courtroom in my blue button-down shirt, my blue slacks and my wingtip shoes. While waiting to hear my case called, I managed to fall asleep. I awoke to the laughter of the dude next to me and a dirty look from the lawyer. My attorney had worked out some kind of deal. They read the charges against me and asked me how I pleaded. I looked over at the lawyer and he mouthed the word "guilty." "Guilty, your Honor."

I was able to keep my license. I paid a $300 fine and was put on probation to not drive like a maniac for the next year. It could have been much worse. As far as the Colt, there were impound fees, a smashed-up front-end and windshield. The old superstition of not driving something you almost died in crept into my brain. Also, I had no true idea of how messed up the car really was. But what really made me upset was that I had about $100 worth of scrap metal in the hatchback of the Colt and I needed that money to get into a new car. Prepared as I was to give the Colt as a gift to the city of Minneapolis, I wanted my scrap.

The impound lot, down off of Dunwoody in Minneapolis, is one of the most vile places on God's green earth. The lost souls line up to deal with these jerks, who relish watching dreams get crushed into smithereens. "No, no help. You can only take what you can carry yourself." Wow. Surely one of these made-up rules made up by assholes. "And you can't take the stereo or the battery."

So I walked through that infernal mud pit of misery and carried, for what seemed like miles and miles, all the scrap metal I could hold in my filthy arms. I loaded it into my buddy's trunk, signed over the car to the city of Minneapolis and said goodbye to the Brown 1981 Dodge Colt.

1986 Toyota Celica

I never fixed this car, but I rode in it quite a bit. It was owned by a manic redhead that just about destroyed me. (Wait, didn't I start another chapter like this?) Anyway, her mother was famous author. The canonized, deep psychological aspects of her esteemed book did not, however, mean her daughter was able to handle relationships. And this chick was fancy East Coast all the way. And I found this exotic.

If I could just make a quick scientific point and speak for my gender... Yes, us the crude, brutish hunter-gatherers who no struggle to clumsily forage upon the urban landscape: We are confused. Because some of our most amazing physical experiences are not with nurturing future mothers and mates for life, no, we have those enthralling moments with girls that can only be described as psychotic.

It was indeed a complicated mess. It was the last time I attempted to have two girls at the same time, even if they were safely placed thousands of miles apart. It is just not healthy. As you can tell, I could barely manage one woman. Now, she may have very well been clinically insane, yet I was no better. I think the technical term is "Drunken Jerk." I was in the "take, take, take" mode of life. And I really have no excuse other than I refused to grow up, and I was a long way from home and confused as hell. She really did give me a proper tour of New England, for damn sure. Because of her mother, she had access to many of the writing and artist colonies scattered about. She had keys to these places and we'd go there when no one was around and have just a torrid drunken romp.

Yet one of the more memorable trips in that hatchback had to be a white-knuckle drive to New York City to see Sonic Youth and Neil Young. We went with our bass player, "The Ox", who began drinking beer in the backseat as soon as we left Northampton. This made our driver even more upset, nervous and insane, but nobody could really stop that guy from doing anything, including me. Also, he had the tickets to the concert. He had somehow befriended Ann Magnuson, the actress, as well as the producer Kramer, who were both in the band Bongwater. So we picked up these ultra-hip New Yorkers somewhere in the East Village. We drove about a mile and Ann Magnuson leaned up from the cramped backseat and whispers into my ear, "Is she on LSD?"

"No," I whispered back.

We finally made it to the Nassau Coliseum on Long Island and we find our excellent seats in the 11th row. I'm told this entire tour with Sonic Youth was Neil Young's idea. But I think it's safe to say that many of Mr. Young's fans are not quite as progressive and experimental as their hero. Sonic Youth received a slightly indifferent, if not hostile, reaction from the crowd. I happen to like heavily distorted bass guitar and people using drumsticks as guitar picks. Also, for noise, it is actually quite beautiful and lovely. Sonic Youth cranks through their set and then Neil Young takes the stage.

This all took place in the middle of the first Gulf War. Neil Young's stage is a bit bizarre. He had a huge yellow ribbon up front for the troops on the microphone stand and then a giant peace sign as the stage backdrop. I guess he wanted it both ways, which you are allowed to do if you are Canadian. He played all of his great tunes and the crowd went wild. I find it rather interesting that when he made a bunch of noise with his guitar, it is "classic," but when Sonic Youth did it, it was noise. Kramer seemed disgusted with the contradiction of the show.

Not only did we have the best seats at an arena rock concert that I've ever had, we also got to go backstage, drink the band's beer and meet the band. They were all very nice. I first went up to Steve Shelly, the drummer. I told him that I was a big fan of the Crucifucks, his punk band from Michigan. We also talked about Die Kruetzen, the legendary band from Milwaukee. Midwestern talk, along with free beer, helped to put me at ease. I finally had the courage to go up and say hi to Kim Gordon. As I approached her, two thoughts hit me at the same time: Wow—she is incredibly hot, and wow—far older than I could have ever imagined. She was also very friendly. She told us about the struggles she had with the jackass Neil Young soundman, some union prick who hated their music and gave them crappy sound. It took an intervention from Neil Young himself to straighten him out.

My massive celebrity weekend just wore me out. After the concert, we crammed into the Celica and got back to Manhattan. The Ox went his way with his celebrity friends, my companion and I went to crash with my buddy who was in NYU law school. I demanded to be the driver on the way back to Northampton, if only for my own safety.

Back in Massachusetts, our relationship sputtered along in fits and starts. It wasn't healthy, but it was highly addictive. One night, the band was playing some after-hours party. She was in the front row, drunk out of her mind, thrashing about. I normally would find this attractive, but for some reason it really bothered me. And even though the band was rocking away and the place was packed, I thought, for the first time in my life, Dear God, I wish the police would raid this party, shut it down and arrest her.

The cops never did arrive, but things just naturally fell apart without the help of law enforcement. The last I heard from her, she called me from an emergency payphone on I-95. The hood had come loose on the Celica and flown up and cracked the windshield. It was at night and she was spooked. And of course, this was all somehow my fault. She was just screaming the F-word at me. I think this made her feel better.

Listening to all this on my official UMass-issued student landline, I was lying on my little single bed in my little graduate school dorm room, feeling like I might as well be on the Soviet Space Station or a nuclear submarine off the coast of China while this tragically beautiful woman yelled obscenities at me from a dark New England freeway. I tried to be practical. I told her to close the hood, get on the hood and stomp on it. Then find some rope or tape in the car, or even some wacky thing she might have in her hair and wrap it around the grill and the hood latch. I don't think she was listening. She just kept cussing. I took the phone and gently returned it to the cradle. I laid back on my bed, stared into the light fixture, and cried.

1976 El Camino

I actually spent almost two long years without any car at all. I arrived at graduate school, dropped off by Mike in his 1984 $75 Toyota Corolla with a bicycle, a cooler, a leather jacket, a U.S. Army duffel bag full of clothes, a suitcase full of punk rock cassettes, a boom box, and $300 in my boot. In my naïve state, I thought I would receive my $5000 fellowship the minute I graced the hallowed halls of the UMass English Department.

No, this was not the case at all, dear reader. In fact, said fellowship was dribbled out to yours truly monthly like some sort of welfare check, a chunk of it drained by bizarre University fees that rivaled the tax rates of a Scandinavian nation. So there I was, a month into my new life as a poet, a "fellow," flipping burgers at a campus coffee shop for student work wages and a free meal. Another shit job didn't really bother me. It conflicted with my idealized dream of a dreamy academic life, but so did most reality.

Yet being away from my friends and family was what brought about my true education. I didn't know a soul in the entire state of Massachusetts. So I began to really read for the first time. I was an early reader as a toddler, shocking my parents by reading billboards out loud as we drove down University Avenue. In high school, I took a speed-reading class. The primitive methods of listening to a cassette and watching words fly by on a screen seemed to work on me. Whilst my bored classmates slid in Led Zeppelin tapes and zoned out, I increased my reading speed to over a thousand words per minute. But I still didn't understand reading.

Junker Dreams

It was in that massive university library, after frying hamburgers and cruising around Amherst on my bicycle aimlessly, that I indeed settled down to learn the power of the written word. My regimen consisted of one rule: No books were to be taken out of the library; they were to be read right then and there. I would spend almost all day at this task. If I didn't finish a book, I would hide it in the stack and get it the next day.

The random wandering of the stacks was also part of my routine, and I warmly recommend it to everyone. It was in those stacks that I put together my program, my pile of reading, my mountain of text to climb. Part of this experience was to read the total works of any given author: Good, bad and ugly, I crept into the skulls of supposed masters. Sometimes I felt like I learned everything and then nothing at the same time. Perhaps all the different styles cancelled themselves out. But I didn't just read literature—I read bizarre technical manuals and plenty of history. And I'm sure I opened up every single art book at the "Tower of Power", my nickname for that place. It was there, one Saturday morning, that I opened a Robert Mapplethorpe book entitled "Women." I found it to be pretty dull stuff until I saw a picture where the book simply stated "Cindy Sherman, 1983." I had discovered her "Untitled Film Stills" back in St. Paul, and I don't really know why I was so struck by them, I just was. So I sat there staring at her rather plain face, the blank canvas for all her photographic stunts and was eerily amazed.

I slowly made friends, but I kept my reading ritual going. And all that reading was great, but I was getting restless. I was used to putting on punk rock shows and tearing scrap metal apart with a crowbar. On my many bicycle trips, even in rural Amherst, I had sighted some scrap. I attempted to explain to my fellow MFA students the scrap metal business. They thought I was nuts. One rather attractive female fiction writer said, "Do you mean to tell me that you would be digging in the garbage?" One of my first real friends there, Jack Mackerel, had no car. But then he said, "Hey, Bill is from Cleveland. And he has some kind of car... pickup type thing." My ears pricked up when I heard the word "Cleveland." I thought, Midwest, industrial, yes! And then I said to Jack, "Do you mean to tell me that this guy has an El Camino?" Shit.

I found Bill sitting in the English Department Lounge. We had an instant connection, and he was kind enough to humor me in my New England scrapping adventure. The problem was that scrap was at an all-time low. The Russians and Brazilians were flooding the market with cheap aluminum. But we did have our share of really good scores. One of Bill's pals was a security guard at a periscope factory in Northampton. He let us in there on the sly and I have never seen so much copper and brass. When the Department of Defense decides to throw stuff away, they don't mess around. All the best scrapping scores are inside jobs. I found us a scrapyard in Belchertown, MA. I was used to the gigantic urban scrapyards of Minneapolis, where it was real easy to get run over by a forklift. When we pulled up, I was shocked. The outfit in Belchertown was one guy and one scale. I asked him what the scrap scene was like in Holyoke and Springfield. "Don't go down there," he said with a grimace. "The Puerto Ricans will kill you."

We had a few other choice scrap grabs with the El Camino. We made some cash and had a great time just driving around and exploring Western Mass. At one point, our rowdy little crew of two stripped all the copper out of an abandoned Greenhouse. I cut my head on a jagged pipe and bled profusely. I went to health services (after we had secured the scrap) and they taped my head up, unconvinced by my bogus explanation that I was "cleaning my basement and I just bumped into something." The nurse sternly told me I could NOT have any painkillers, even though I never asked for them. Back in the UMass English Dept, James Tate, the Pulitzer Prize winning poet who was my advisor, pulled me aside one day. "What's this I hear about you and Bill tearing the town apart with a crowbar?" He pretended he was concerned, but I could tell that it brought him a special joy. "Just keeping the town a tidy place, trying to do my part," I said. Tate just raised his eyebrows and walked away, chuckling under his breath.

One day Bill and I were behind the appliance repair shop in Northampton, doing some real meager scrapping—ripping out drop cord and little bits of copper. Bill just said, in a timely fashion, "Where have all the good times gone?" And so, with all the big scores gone, we gave up on the scrapping. Yet Bill's generosity with the car didn't end there. He drove myself and a fiction writer from the MFA program named Chip and some of my gear down to Boston for a gig at the Middle East. One the way back to Northampton, after dropping Chip off in Amherst, a cop tailed us all the way down Route 9, for what seemed like an eternity. He finally pulled us over. We heard him report the El Camino on the radio as a "suspicious vehicle." He separated Bill and I and interrogated us. Playing music at a club in Boston was evidently some sort of crime. There was some BS regarding Bill's insurance, and the bastards towed the El Camino and impounded it. We were left at the side of the road with a Peavey TNT 130 bass amp and two guitars.

1985 Ford E-150

This van, this van, this van! Dear Lord, I am a pathetic creature. I am pond scum. I am sea plankton. I am a Neanderthal, a reprobate. I drove this truck back to Massachusetts. I was entering my final year of Graduate Study. I should have been concentrating on my thesis. Or getting together my lesson plans for the South Boston jarheads I had to babysit as a teaching assistant. But no, I was obsessed with a girl. I knew something was wrong. In a man's deluded mind, he thinks he can do something, he thinks he can save himself, convince the girl to change her mind. I may be living proof that this myth is indeed bullshit. And what was it about her? That she was oh so slightly out of reach? That she went to Yale and was a fine specimen of WASP decadence? Dear Van, you are truly my only friend.

I drove. I drove 26 hours straight. I slept through 70 miles of Indiana and didn't hit a thing. I was awakened by some honking, so I got off at a rest stop. I put my head under a sink. I slapped myself. I then looked at the giant map at the rest stop. I had no memory of that last hour or so that I ate up on that map. Am I a fool that has cheated death? Yes. Am I still a fool? Yes.

I rolled into Northampton, about 8am on a Saturday morning. It was my brilliant idea to go straight to her house. Well, I was in for a surprise. As a man, I guess this has to happen once in your life and I hope that I have used up my turn. Yes, Northampton is a sleepy town, where people don't lock their doors. So I walk in and find her in bed with a guy. Wow.

Not cool. What is your next move? Do you get a gun and shoot the bastard? Hmm... Or do you run out of there and go to the only place that can really soothe the soul? That is what I did. Not that the twerp didn't deserve to be shot, but I deserved a life sentence in a federal prison just slightly less. I ended up at that special spot, but it wasn't open, so I hung out on the dock of the Smith College Boathouse. I really liked that pond—you could check out a boat with a UMass ID, go sit in the middle of the pond and do absolutely nothing. That day I just sat on the dock and cried.

I was walking, but I felt like I was crawling up to Pleasant Street to get on my favorite payphone. I called collect to a girl named Ann Miller, an artist. I had her number memorized. I pictured her in her cluttered apartment on Selby Avenue, eating Ramen and smoking cigarettes. I found that image so soothing. Somehow this weird creature talked me slightly back to sanity. I spilled my story. She told me that I wasn't a loser. Then she asked me a simple question: "When is the last time you ate or slept?" I really had no answer. I thanked her. By that time the bagel/coffee shop was open. I got a bagel with cream cheese and tomato and a bottle of Orangina. I wolfed it down, walked back to the van, and slept a rough and shallow sleep.

Obviously, no one should take advice from me. But allow me to state that counting on women for your housing is a bad idea. My relationship was over, and I was supposed to shack up with her. It was just me and Mr. Van. I parked in various driveways of friends, or on sleepy side streets. I was homeless for about a month. I relied upon the kindness of others. I slept on a few couches, used a few showers. I taught my freshman English class. I wrote some crappy poems, crumpled them up, threw them in the public trash on Pleasant Street. I kept it together by falling apart. I went to quite a few parties in Northampton. I was the random partygoer. I needed those parties. I drank and danced, met no one in particular, and I didn't care.

I finally found a place—22 Graves Street—with some roommates. It was a little room on the second floor of a drafty, creaky row house. The address meant that it was 22 doors down from the graveyard. There are some things I did love about New England. I later ended up falling for a blonde undergrad art student. We made out on the roof of the Chinese restaurant on Pleasant Street on a beautiful day. I brought her down to the Smith Boathouse, we checked out a rowboat, and we sat in the middle of that damn pond. She had her room in an old house and I had mine. And I didn't burn down the town of Northampton or shoot anyone after all.

Ford E-150

1988 VW Golf Convertible

They say that a car says quite a bit about the driver. For the most part, I think this is bunk. In my case, I was driving whatever I could get my hands on for little or nothing, so the make and model was a random factor. But if you were a hot blonde, and your dad takes you to a car lot, you might pick out a fun car that expresses your personality, like the VW Golf. This isn't Europe. If you want to go out on a date with a girl, you get your hands on a machine. Every male can't wait to turn sixteen and get on the road.

Yet there is something so special about the girl doing the driving. Especially if she is a 22 year old art student and she is pulling up to 22 Grave Street with the top down. She was wild, and I mean that as a high, sacred and loving compliment. She wasn't crazy. She got a little mean when she was ripped on wine, but nobody is perfect. As I sit here, I realize I am the crazy one for making her just another bittersweet memory. What my real problem was, I guess I will never know. But when it worked, it really worked—I was older—I guess she liked me because I could finish a sentence.

And I met her in the best possible way, I saw her on the UMass campus and gave her a handbill to my band's show. There we were, rocking away at the Baystate in Northampton and I looked up and saw her young, fresh face. I woke up the next morning with her and my Ibanez guitar in my bed. What is romance? I think it is four things. 1) Doing cool shit together. 2) Talking. You talk together for hours about any damn thing, nonstop and the time just flies on by. 3) Sex. 4)

Timing. We were just there, together in Northampton, with a lot of time on our hands.

I had a tiny office in the basement of the English building. As teaching assistants, we were not supposed to have sex with our students. In fact, things were so touchy back then, we were supposed to have our door OPEN at all times. And I did shut the door just that once, but that was to have sex with a certain female MFA candidate. I reasoned that since we were both graduate students and teachers, it was OK. And once, when the art student came by, I wanted to close that door again, get her on the desk and do it on that pile of lame puppy dog essays I was correcting. Yes, she was a student, but not MY student. For God's sake, I was in the English, not the Art department! Alas, I sit here with regret at my foolish restraint.

Timing. Yes, so essential regarding romance. Sometimes it cannot survive a change of scenery. That summer I visited her and her 88 VW GOLF in the Boston suburb of Newton for a long weekend. And during this visit I played a different role, that of the longhaired dirt bag older boyfriend that the parents didn't like. I mean, I didn't even try to be liked. This, of course, made her like me more and I was, much to my amazement, allowed to spend the night in her bedroom, a charming Victorian cupola. But towards the end of the visit, things did get a bit strained. It was too late to charm the liberal yet resistant parents, and as her fling—her experiment—I simply had reached my expiration date.

And so I returned to St. Paul to run the gallery and attempt to write poetry for the rest of my life. My MFA diploma arrived at my P.O. box about a month later. This is the same P.O. box I have had since I was sixteen—I set it up to sell punk rock cassettes on the back page of *Maximum Rock N Roll Magazine*. I sat down on the curb outside the post office and openly wept as Northampton memories, some good and some bad, rained down upon me in the humid St. Paul heat.

Like all people who are blonde and have Scandinavian heritage, the artist had relatives in Minnesota. So one day she just walked in the front door of the gallery. This being my own business, I was allowed to welcome her into my office and close the door as well. We fell into each other's arms quickly, as if nature had not skipped a beat. I knew it would not or could not last, but a visit is a visit and you need to show some hospitality. I am clearly a fool, and my kingdom has been lost many times. Yet if I were to be truly honest, and I owe you that, dear reader, I would have to say that the legacy of that whole affair that is emblazed upon my mind, was how perfect and lovely her young breasts were, accented with a new, tiny skull tattoo between them. And, as a man, perhaps I am indeed ready to meet my maker now, to flip my car over on I-94 and cash in my chips, because she shared their sweet perfection with me and I learned what it was like to truly be alive.

Dodge Astro Van

1981 White Dodge Colt

Strange pathways led me to this car. It all started with a pretty girl and a BMW 2002. Now, the BMW 2002 is just about the coolest car ever made. Boxy, tiny and full of power and Euro-trash flair, it is one of my favorites. I've never owned one. Mike had a yellow one he paid $400 for. He drove down to Mexico and back in that thing. What a total madman. Now, if a BMW 2002 is the coolest car, a Dodge Colt is perhaps one of the dorkiest cars. I was, however, convinced there was a cult surrounding the Colt, namely because once some African guy at a parking garage in Minneapolis yelled at me, "Yes! Dodge Colt!" in some sort of stately accent. The deal is, a Dodge Colt isn't going to help you with the ladies. If a girl wants you because you drive a Dodge Colt, I suggest you marry her immediately and start procreating.

I wasn't attempting to procreate, just kill the loneliness that lived inside me. I've got nothing against going to rehab. Some people need it. But if you told me that I had to go to just one meeting, I would fly straight pretty damn quick. Rehab is big business in the state of Minnesota. We have treatment centers that draw people from all over the world.

Here name was Alex. She was a tall brunette with a strange accent from Toronto. I had opened up the seized carburetor on her BMW, but I wanted to do oh so much more. In my pursuit of the sophisticated Alex, however, I realized something a bit scary. Except for some innocent make-out sessions in high school, every one of my romances involved booze. I needed some "Irish Courage" to make any moves. And so, in a long blue-balled haze of missed opportunities, I hung out with Alex and didn't try a goddamn thing.

Alex was friends with Kelly Deal of the rock band The Breeders. Kelly is the sister of Kim Deal, also of said Breeders. Kim is the bassist for the Pixies and many men of my age have had crazed fantasies about Kim Deal. I liked Kelly's gentle spirit. I tried to sell her a Toyota 4Runner, but the tailgate wouldn't open, so I can't blame her for not buying it. Turned out it was for the best, since I traded it to the Mexican girl at the gas station for free gas.

Kelly had a roommate where she lived down on Grand Avenue. This roommate wanted to sell me his Dodge Colt for $100. Some people have faces—he might have had one, but I cannot remember it. I know he wore a baseball cap. I showed up unannounced one day with $75 cash. He had the key and the title and I was on my way.

The car was a winner. It had a manual transmission and was really a blast to drive. I found an American flag decal and stuck it right on the quarter panel, like I was an official member of the team USA rally race team. I drove that damn car everywhere. I ran a thousand crazed missions. That little Mitsubishi in-line-4-banger engine had plenty of power. I felt invincible.

While I was Captain of the Dodge Colt, they tore down the old Buick dealership on Fairview and University in St. Paul. They didn't have the site fenced off. I just rolled in with the Colt right after the demo dust had settled. There was a dude with a hardhat there. He was actually friendly. "Hey, what is the scene with the scrap here?" I asked in a tentative manner.

"Well, they just want to get rid of all this shit, so have at it. You probably have about a half an hour before the black guys come back for more." Ah, yes, I thought, the black guys in the green truck, my spirited competitors in the scrap trade. And have at it, I did, filling that Colt hatchback so full of aluminum and copper pipe and brass fittings that I could barely shift and steer.

The next morning I awoke, put on my pants, got a cup of coffee at the Dunn Bros on Snelling and Grand, and drove as fast as that little car would take me on I-94 to the scrapyard in Northeast Minneapolis. Everyone at the yard was entertained when I careened in there, defying the laws of physics. If I would have had an accident, I would have been decapitated. I made $434 in pure, tax-free cash.

Perhaps I should have followed the lovely Alex into a life of sobriety. Yet it all seemed like so much work, admitting you have problems. The truth is, I really didn't like drinking that much, yet I found it an essential ingredient to romance, so yes, indeed, I am less than perfect, but not much of a danger to others. I was just a guy a $75 car who really wasn't ready to grow up.

I was in Minneapolis, doing my thing. I sold some books in Uptown and I then I hustled downtown to get a free meal from my friend Nancy at the New French Café. I took Lasalle into South Minneapolis and sold some records at a record store. The clutch was really starting to slip. I resolved to make my way back to St. Paul on Lake Street. If there was one street for driving damaged cars, it was Lake Street. The clutch was fading fast. As I crossed Chicago Avenue, the deathwatch on the clutch truly began. I cursed every red light, as I was barely able to slam the thing into gear and get it moving. But I did.

I felt a sense of triumph as I crossed the Mississippi on the Lake Street Bridge. Yet as I entered St. Paul, my situation deteriorated. As I attempted to trot up the Marshall hill toward Cretin Avenue, the clutch finally just disappeared. The Colt began sliding backward, with no gear in the gearbox that would engage. My hazard lights had been on since I hit the bridge, so luckily no other car was right on my tail. I was able to slide into a parking spot on Marshall. As fun as it was, being part of the Dodge Colt captive import cult, I knew it was time to say goodbye. Seven months for $75 was a good deal.

So there I was again. No car, no girl, walking home without a plan, and not making any plans at all.

1991 Ford Taurus

For some reason that no one can really explain to me, I went through a period of time when lesbian couples were giving me cars. (Well, the first one I had to buy for $40, but I guess I consider that free.)

In all business transactions, inside information is invaluable. I worked with a girl named Dana at the Chinese restaurant. We got along well. One night, she was in a really good mood. She revealed to me that her girlfriend was getting a brand-new VW Jetta from her parents and that they had this old Ford Taurus that didn't work. This Taurus was a classic case of asshole mechanical foolishness, but it actually worked in my favor at this time. Dana took it in to the garage and these meatheads told her that one of the pistons was shot and that it would cost $1,500. I won't even get into the entire "piston repair" absurdity, but the cost alone (why don't most garages realize this?) means no repair, no business, and a guy like me takes over.

I drove the car for three minutes and I knew that the diagnosis was bogus. This car had a perfect body and the interior was mint. The temp gauge shot up like a rocket. I knew it was just a case of overheating. Dana was sitting on the porch, smoking a cigarette, when I pulled up after my little test-drive. "Yeah, it's pretty messed up, but I can take if off your hands." This was my classic line. I tried not to seem too interested, but I was practically salivating over this car. They had to think about it.

Junker Dreams

A week later I was on a bicycle ride and I rode past the duplex and saw the new Jetta sitting in the driveway. These girls liked to party, so I hatched a plan. Sometimes you need to use the 18th century technology called "showing up." I purchased a bottle of tequila and put two $20 bills in my pocket, got on my bike and rode over there. I knocked on the door. They were a bit surprised, but they let me in. As I guessed, they were in celebration mode over the new German automobile. I offered up the tequila and we all did a shot. "So, what's with the Taurus?" Dana replied that it wouldn't even start. This worked in my favor. "Well, that car needs a lot of work, but I have to give you something." It was then that I offered them my $40. Cash, even in that paltry amount, is an excellent visual stimulant. She gave me the key. I left the tequila on the table.

I knew I could get it to start, but I didn't want to start it in front of them—this could ruin my entire deal. I messed around under the hood, muttering abstract mechanical BS until they got bored and went upstairs. The battery cable was loose, so I tightened it with my fingers. I threw the bike in the trunk, started the beast and drove away like a maniac.

The Taurus and I sailed into the closest gas station, the Super America on Snelling and Englewood. I never liked their gas—they water it down, it is real crap. But I liked their cheap pastries. I really needed a doughnut and the Taurus needed some coolant. God knows what antifreeze really is. All I truly know is that dogs like the taste, but it can kill them. I'll apologize to all the doggies right now for all the machines that have leaked the green liquid. But the Taurus wasn't one of them—the car was overheating because THERE WAS NOT A DROP OF COOLANT in the radiator! "Blown piston" indeed.

This is one car I truly wish I still owned. It was a real sleeper. I became a proud Taurus driver. I discovered that the fatal flaw of the Taurus was the automatic transmission failure. But this amazing sedan had a stick and it was fast as hell. I let my brother drive it a few times to work in Plymouth and he loved it. I let my dad use it and he had so much fun with it he got a speeding ticket on I-94.

O, the Mighty Taurus. At this point in my life, I was addicted to flipping cars. All I could see were dollar signs. So far this car cost me Forty U.S. Dollars, a jug of coolant and a cheap bottle of Jose Cuervo. It is a game: How little can you spend? How much can you make? Welcome to America! I was visualizing a wad of money rolled up in my pocket. But I started to like the car too much, to get attached—dangerous sentiment if you want to make money. Because every car is a rolling time bomb; every minute it creeps toward the junkyard with a trail of repairs and cash spent along the way. Eventually it needed break work. Mr. V helped me do the brakes, but it killed me to spend (gasp) $100 in parts and labor, plus a pizza.

Once the brakes were done, I received a call that my family needed the car. Well, a good Irish boy from St. Paul always knows what to do—he brings over the car. On my way over, tooling down University Avenue with my brand-new brakes, everything changed. Right as I'm considering an impromptu visit to the White Castle on Lexington Parkway, a zippy new Honda comes out of nowhere and T-bones me. I guess he was trying to zoom across Dunlap Street into the Bally's gym.

I got popped and spun around. In every accident I've ever been a part of, my primary concern was the car. When my little 180-dgree dance was over, I was just enraged that the car wouldn't start! This freaked me out more than anything. It was later that I learned that the Taurus has a kill switch installed to halt the car upon sudden impact. But I was so thrilled, because I realized that for once in my life, this accident was NOT MY FAULT. I hopped out and saw that the body was really OK. Honda Boy just managed to cave in my driver's side rear tire. He started yelling about me being in the wrong lane—I just laughed in his face.

Dude's Honda is pretty well munched, I've never been so thrilled to involve law enforcement in my entire life. I ran across University Avenue and call the police on a payphone. I went back to the accident scene and Mr. Honda still has a fantasy about my mythical lane. "Ok," I told I him, "Let's just see what the cops say." Well, the police did not let me down. I got a carbon copy of the police report that favored me and I was ready to take this to the Supreme Court if I had to. I got the Taurus towed to the most expensive repair shop I can think of. This place has been fleecing the people of St. Paul for years. I'm sure that they have boats, lake homes and Harley Davidson motorcycles to prove it.

The bill for repairs is, of course, absurd. It is way beyond the Blue Book value of the car. It is totaled. The insurance company is going to cut me a check for $1,000. Seems like a great deal, right? Not good enough for me.

There is a certain breed of arrogant jackass mechanic/manager butthead types at these body shops. There was a certain breed of arrogant punk rock underground backyard mechanics such as myself. We didn't get along too well. So Mr. V and I went down to the great auto body palace. I have to pay them $70 for their brilliant analysis. Then I ask them for the key. "Oh," the man in a polo with feathered hair told me, "you can't drive away the car, it's totaled."

"Oh yeah? It is my property. I want it back." I'm pretty sure they are not used to people who want to drive away a car with a caved-in wheel. He pontificated with a know-it-all sneer.

"It is against the law. I can't let you drive that car away." He acted like this was a war crime tribunal. What a scam. We stared at each other. I was to launch into a crazed tirade when reason prevailed.

"OK." We left in a huff.

Always make multiple copies of your car key. Same day, 11:30pm, Mr. V and I went back to the shop parking lot. He got underneath the Taurus, messed with the axle. He was a true genius. I was a hack. He somehow got the wheel a bit straighter. I was getting extremely nervous. What if they didn't reset the accident kill switch? I got in the car. It started right up.

I limped the Taurus back to the bat cave. The next day we fixed it proper. It was like the entire thing never happened, except that I was getting a check. The police never came looking for me because I had stolen my own car. Now, I didn't mind driving cars around where parts might fly off at high speeds or collapse or catch on fire at given moment, but I'd of felt bad if that happened to my next of kin, so I didn't let my family have the post-accident car. My solution: Sell it.

Back at my job, where, as you can tell, most of my car transactions occurred , there was a new heavy metal dishwasher. I will always defend the dishwasher's right to listen to ear-splitting heavy metal. If you have ever had that job, you understand. His name was Randy. Randy was saving up money for a trip back to his hometown of Appleton, Wisconsin. He was looking for some wheels. I showed him the Taurus and he fell in love. I took a liking to this kid. I wanted him to go back to his town in the understated middle-class elegance of the Mighty Taurus. We worked out a payment plan. I came clean about the jacked back-end. He shrugged. I set the price at $700. Every couple of weeks we'd meet at Cosmic Charlie's coffee shop on Snelling and he'd give me at least $100. He lost count and tried to pay me more than the $700. It was a business ethics test. I told him he was done with his payments. Randy informed me, sitting in the endless cigarette smoke of that coffee shop, that he and his girlfriend, a seemingly mute Goth chick, are taking that trip back to Appleton.

Randy quit the dishwashing job. I wished him luck and figured I'll never see him again. About two months later, I stop in to get a cup of coffee and there is Randy with his lady Goth.

"So, Randy, how's the Taurus running?" I asked in an All-American, aw shucks way.

"Some old lady ran a red light and hit us pretty hard. It was totaled. We got a check for $1,000." I peered through the cigarette haze, trying to figure out how far away Appleton, Wisconsin was.

"Wow," I said. And then I asked him, "Just how 'totaled' was it?"

I could tell he knew I was thinking of going and trying to grab the Taurus again, of trying to keep the drama alive. Randy just flashed me a smile and walked away.

1983 Renault Alliance

I got this car from the right-wing lesbians I met at the Turf Club. One of them looked like she was right out of the '40s, so I gave her a vintage purse. A friend of mine said to me that night, "Dude, I don't know what you are up to, but I saw her and her girlfriend making out at the Tribe 8 show." Oh, well, no matter. We became fast friends. They claimed to have a French car in their garage. I was intrigued. "A Peugot?" No. "A Citroen?" No. "Le Car?" No.

It turned out that it was really a beat Renault Alliance, the French car that was actually built in Kenosha, Wisconsin. The Alliance was designed to break into the American market. I don't think this ever happened because the only person who seemed to end up with these tin cans was me. Renault bought AMC, the company that brought the world the Javelin, a damn cool muscle car that actually had a Pierre Cardin interior (so much cooler than Eddie Bauer) as well as the Pacer and the Gremlin. The Alliance is a no-frills car. It was based on the popular French 9/09. It featured a buggy-type ride, constricted handling and little pep. And this particular unit had some whack problems that took quite a while to figure out. The left rear tire was so rusted that it was completely seized. After beating it with a hammer for an hour to get it loose, I took everything apart—the brake, the drum, the tire. I scrubbed the whole mess with a wire brush and soaked everything in gasoline. I felt like I was working on a damn bicycle.

Another issue: The car would start, yet would not shift into reverse. I tried it again and again. I crawled under there and discovered one of the most idiotic things I've ever seen. A piece of wire, used to hold up the exhaust, was blocking the linkage and keeping the selector from shifting the gears. This car had the mechanical dynamics of an erector set, but at least it was repairable by someone with my limited skills.

So I took many trips to that ramshackle garage in Frogtown, to drink beer with the gals and work on the French car with the 1397cc engine made famous by Le Car, assembled in Wisconsin and reassembled by me in St. Paul.

Now, I can hate Commies, taxes and city inspectors as much as the next person, but these ladies were really into it. To appease them, I gave them the now hard-to-find Barry Goldwater autobiography and the obligatory selection of Ayn Rand paperbacks. They were, of course, well-armed. I think someone tried to rob them once and they were met with a hail of bullets. From then on, they were left in peace. What I saw of their arsenal was a shotgun and a Colt .45 Automatic. This was not only for home defense, but it was their God-given right to bear arms. They always referred to people as "collectivist," which was uttered as a certain insult.

As strident as they were in their political beliefs, they were OK people. I thought they were valuable people to know. If I really needed to vanish for a while, if I truly needed to be safe, I felt I could just go hide out with the right-wing lesbians. I didn't know them very well, but I trusted them. They were well armed and I'm sure they could keep a secret. Isn't that the definition of a real friend?

This entire time I thought I was just fixing this car for them and that they would give me a hundred bucks or something. But they just up and gave me the car. It turned out to be a fun little ride. I parked the Volvo and let it rest for a while. I drove that Alliance around with no insurance, bad tabs and a broken headlight for only three months, which I considered totally reasonable at the time. Sensing that my luck might run out, I sold the Renault to a rocker chick for $300. She had a good run with it until someone bashed out the driver's side window in Northeast Minneapolis. I recall making a half-assed attempt to look for a window at area junkyards. And then I remember nothing at all.

Ford Taurus

1977 Dodge Sportsman Van

This machine wasn't a Volvo, but it got me knee-deep in the Volvo world. It involved the "Old Man" Volvo. I never bought a Volvo from him, but I did get a few parts and learn a few tricks from the "Old Man." We called him this because, well, we were in our early twenties and he was in his seventies. This guy was a mechanical genius. He was also a decorated war hero—he was given a Navy Cross in WWII. In the 1950's he invented some part for the vacuum cleaner and made a huge pile of money. He owned a house out on Lake Minnetonka and several classy boats.

Then he drank it all away. For those of you unfamiliar with this phenomenon, give it a few years. So around 1974, he ends up in an old insurance storefront on Selby Avenue. He told me that he bought it for $4,000 cash. That is a figure that will stick in my head forever. His compound consisted of the single-story insurance office building, which still had the old gold lettering from the defunct insurance agency on the big shop window. In the storefront, there was a front office, a kitchen and another room with a Murphy bed. Behind the building were several ramshackle garages full of Volvos and Volvo parts. It was all fenced in, urban-fortress style, with a drawbridge-style flip-up gate.

We became his neighbors when my friends and I opened up an art gallery/underground rock club in our own decrepit storefront next door. He had a repair license from the city, but I don't think that fire hazard and hazmat zone was ever inspected. The Old Man's deal was selling Volvos. He would get them, fix them up and sell them. The entire neighborhood, in a five-block radius, was scattered with Volvos. His entire business was based upon a tiny ad that he ran in the St. Paul *Pioneer Press* Classifieds that simply stated: "I will repair or buy your old Volvo (612) 647-9733."

He was character that was fun to watch in action. He was good at getting the cars for nothing and selling them for an insane price. Every dealing I had with him, he got the upper hand. It didn't matter what sort of transaction it was, I felt ripped off. But the Old Man was OK—he was one of us, a member of the underground, living illegally in a storefront on a stretch of city street that was, at that time, forgotten. Just to mess with people, we often had him take the door cover at the punk rock shows. These hipsters would show up and this 72-year guy who looked like Ed McMahon would demand $5. What's more punk than that?

A few of my friends worked for him over the years—getting cars, doing mechanical work, selling some cars. They usually quit after a while, resulting from some sort of financial dispute. I remember one guy claiming the Old Man tried to pay him in pies from Bakers Square. But I was always on good terms with him, for whatever reason. Long after my business had been shut down by the St. Paul Police and Fire Department, the Old Man was still in his compound, plugging away, fixing and flipping those cars.

I was riding my bicycle past there one day and I stopped to chat. "Say," he said, "do you want to come work for me?" I really did not, so I just sat on my bike and smiled. He had a Cadillac in the driveway. He was working to fix the adjustable electric seats, one of the many frills that make a Caddy a Caddy. So I did give him a hand, pushing the buttons while he messed with the wiring. After he figured it out, he thanked me and I was on my way.

About two weeks later, I heard that the Old Man had passed away. He must have been in his early 80s. The dearly departed had one steady employee. This dude, named Doug, was one of the best mechanics I've ever met. He was the one person that the Old Man never ripped off—hell or high water, Doug got paid in cash every week. Tooling down Selby Avenue, I saw Doug in front of the Old Man's place. Doug was a rather stoic fellow, but he came to life when he saw my cargo van. This rig was pretty damn awesome. It was what was called a "stubby"—meaning that it was just ¾ the size of a regular van. I bought it from some weirdo out in Lake Elmo for $250. It had a 3-speed on the floor that was a real bitch to get into gear. You really had to stomp on the clutch, and it worked best if you wore combat boots. It was light blue, slightly rusty, and it had mirrored windows. It had two bucket seats and then it was all Mopar steel—pure cargo space. It was like a miniature C-130 cargo plane. Damn, I wish it was parked out back right now.

The Sportsman had an 8-track player with *Goat's Head Soup* by the Rolling Stones in the deck. I never took it out, I just played it over and over in the player. I had a theory that it kept the van running. So just as I'm hearing "Angie" for the millionth time, I pulled in the little driveway where the Caddy had been. "Sorry to hear about the Old Man," I tell Doug.

"Yeah," Doug taps the side of the van. "Is this what you are driving now?"

I nodded. "That's right."

"Well, the family"—I guess the Old Man had grown children none of us ever saw—"is letting me scrap all the parts. Do you want to help?"

That was one damn hot summer. We tried to start at about 6am and left for the scrapyard by noon. Doug was a great scrapping partner because he knew how to use tools. The more you break down your metal, the more money you make. It needs to be broken down into all the nonferrous categories: Copper, Aluminum, Stainless Steel, and Brass. Volvo engines and transmissions are full aluminum. And many of the cars had catalytic converters with a honeycomb of actual platinum in them, making them extremely valuable.

Doug knew which of the transmissions still worked, so we were able to sell them to a Volvo shop in Minneapolis. With a cargo van, pretty much damn anything is possible. I was willing to go 60/40 because Doug lost his job. Yet he insisted we do 50/50 because none of this could be happening without the Sportsman van. 50/50 is usually the way to go anyway—it is simple and it keeps morale high. And we needed all the positive morale we could get, throwing around engines and transmissions in 90-degree heat.

I insisted on going all the way to Northeast Minneapolis to sell the scrap. I never liked the scrapyards in St. Paul. They were just jerks and they always tried to rip you off. That van would be so loaded down with scrap that the front-end was almost airborne as we tooled down I-94. We would try to hit the yard every day, so we could get that cash in our pockets. The thinking was that we would be inspired to get up at 6 the next morning for more oil-soaked filth and heavy lifting. Sometimes I gave Doug a ride to where he lived in Blaine. The first time I pulled up to his double-wide trailer he looked at me and said, in a sort of post-modern stoicism, "Yeah, I live in one of these."

That tough-ass little van was a champ. When your truck is what makes you a living, you really develop a special bond, a man-to-machine codependence. It was these underground experiences that kept me from getting a normal life. Just when I'd be ready to give in, to go get a day job, some deal would come my way, and normal life was put on hold again. And this gig was my legend, my cut after it was all said and done, for about a month of work, was $3,000, tax-free cash. For a single guy, who lived in low-rent paradise, this was a windfall. I didn't party with it. I didn't go out and buy a bunch of guitars. I just put it under my mattress and pretended it wasn't there.

Dolan needed a way to move out to NYC. U-Haul is a total scam. I sold him the Sportsman for $400 cash. He and his girlfriend put all their stuff in their truck and moved out to Harlem. Later, the brakes fried out on the van and he sold it to his roommate who was a carpenter in NYC. The last I heard it was sitting on blocks out on Long Island.

Chevy Impala

1982 Volvo 242 DL Sedan

After my little accident with the college girl, my insurance rates soared. I was paying as much as someone with a DWI, by my calculations. Insurance was invented by the British as a way to cover the risks of their merchant fleet. How this degenerated into a corporate scam that preyed upon an unlucky guy with an old car, I'll leave to the historians and economists to sort out.

But now, dear reader, let us trace this car's many mutations. First, it was a dull and cracked Volvo, baby-poop brown. I minted it out with some sweet BMW metallic grey paint and drove it around town like I was hot stuff. Then I got creamed right on Selby Avenue. They say that a car is never the same after an accident. Whoever the hell "they" happen to be 100 percent correct in this instance. My front suspension was jacked. The engine just wanted to go go go, but the ride was a bit goofy and my quarter panel was munched.

There was a junkyard in Rosemount, Minnesota, called "U Pull It." This is the only junkyard I know of where you have to pay a cover to get into the place. For a while, it was famous for its "Euro-trash" and its collection of Mercedes, Volvo, VW, and BMW wrecks. Aside from the cover charge, it was far cheaper than any junkyard in the city and they actually let you pull the parts off. Most junkyards today don't allow that. I went down there with my 10-millimeter ratchet and took of a million little bolts to get a new quarter panel and a bunch of trim parts. I replaced the quarter panel. I had grand plans to bring my machine back to its former glory.

But then it happened. I met another girl.

My band performed at a massive art party in Northeast Minneapolis. It was one of the best shows we ever played. Every man rocks in a band to meet girls. I have been in a band since I was fifteen and it is the only social life I know. It is a terrible sign if a woman doesn't love Rock 'n' Roll. You wait for the right moment, when the band is really kicking ass, you look up from your guitar and she is there. You never expect it—you can't expect it or it will never happen.

So there she is. A beautiful redhead that actually used to be a model. We talked. Well, mainly I talked. Amazing woman—all the world falls to the wayside, the entire world could be on fire. I didn't care. I saw one thing, and there was only one thing: her lovely face. We then proceed to the after-party in the neighborhood. We had a great time and I hitch a ride in her Celica GT back to the Volvo. And then I proceeded to forget to get her phone number. This only added to the drama.

A poem of mine was published in an anthology called *The Poetic Guide to the Twin Cities.* Minnesota Public Radio called. I made the reporter meet me at a walking bridge over I-94. This bridge was in the heart of Frogtown. It was favored by drug dealers, Hmong gangs, strange kids on BMX bicycles, and me.

The Celica had a broken tape deck. Because of that broken tape deck, she tuned in the radio and heard me.

I wrote for an alternative weekly called the *Pulse of the Twin Cities.* I did CD reviews, rock band interviews and various smartass essays. She sent me a letter that actually included her phone number. The letter kicked around the office for a month before anyone told me about it. I was upset, to say the least. But I now understand I was just so lucky those hippies didn't lose the letter or just throw it away. We played a little phone tag and on a Saturday night in July, I carefully parked my car in front of her apartment on Saratoga Street. At this point, I had a quarter panel of a different color, so I parked it with the good side facing the building. She buzzed me in. I went inside and never left.

I couldn't believe my luck. After so many years of loneliness, desperation and alienation, I had found someone. But I was like the lost wolf boy. I had spent so much time out in the wild, living like a savage, that it wasn't easy adjusting to civilization.

Early on, I remember partying with some of the party girls at the Loring Bar. It was what I did to hide from myself. I suddenly realized that it had gotten really late and that she was waiting for me. I left abruptly and got on the highway. I got off at the Snelling exit, took a right and headed south. Somewhere around Portland Avenue, I started crying and then bawling like a child. It got so intense that I could barely drive, and I've had quite a bit of experience driving and crying. I pulled into a church parking lot and continued sobbing. Dear God, I thought— have I fallen in love?

Ford Thunderbird

1978 Ford Thunderbird

This car belonged to the "Old Boy," an eccentric Yankee poet than always referred to himself in the third person. He was from Milford, Connecticut. He, Jack Mackerel and I became fast friends. This friendship was bonded over many drinks and salutations and plans to change the world with our amazing writing.

OB was real tight-lipped. He always wore Converse low-tops and a windbreaker year-round. I loved riding in his T-Bird. It had plush interior and those cool flip-up headlights. It was a nice big car—you felt like you were riding a couch down the road. OB spoke in a cryptic code that took a while to figure out. I'd ask him when he was coming by to get me and he'd say, "As long as a 45 record, B-side." And there was nothing like going into McDonald's and hearing him say, "The Old Boy would like a Big Mac with French fries." The cashier would look a bit confused and then just figure it out. Because he didn't talk very much, his utterances were rather mythical. We were once lost on the Jersey Turnpike, which is a special ring of hell where you can see Manhattan, and you really can't do much about it because you are lost and confused. While everyone was freaking out in the T-Bird, the Old Boy just waved at the skyline and said, "Let's just... get into that city." And we did.

A drinking bender can indeed be educational. Even though we were fleeing our graduate studies back at UMass, there was much learn on the streets of New York. This was pre-Giuliani New York, when people could afford to live in Manhattan. You could also walk down the street past a cop with a tallboy in a paper sack. But I'm from the heartland, so I won't pretend to know much about NYC, other than the bizarre Disneyland it became for me. This particular trip turned into a marathon of staggering late nights and emptiness. That is what you do in New York, especially if you are broke and don't really have a place to go. You just walk around. But the real education of the bender was when to end the bender. It is a moment of utmost clarity. It is not when you are at the beginning, full of promise and frivolity. No, it is at the dear end, when you call some sort of truce with the world. On that particular research expedition with the Old Boy, our moment came one bright spring morning, drinking whiskey out of Dixie cups in Washington Square Park with some Puerto Rican gentlemen. It was only polite to share, and it was only prudent to quit, to quit while you can almost pretend you are ahead of the game.

1985 Dodge Caravan

For almost an entire summer, I worked for a slumlord who owned about 50 buildings all over St. Paul. He was too cheap to pay onsite caretakers, so he hired people to go around and do all the work on the buildings. The jerk-off would turn anyone into a hardcore Communist. He owned many Section 8 properties. Section 8 is a voucher system of subsidized housing. This means the slumlord could not only get paid an over-market rate for his properties, he could also feel superior to the poor people in his buildings.

I liked construction work. And I didn't mind the painting and the lawn mowing. But the insufferable demands and attitude of this arrogant jackass were really too much to bear. Every week I would want to quit, but then every week I would get paid and would hang on just a bit longer.

It was on this job that I met a guy named Peter. Peter was in his fifties and he looked just like Santa Claus. People would tell him that and he would say, "Well, I have ridden with angels... Hell's Angels!" What that had to do with Christmas, I really didn't quite understand. The thing was, Peter was no tough guy, he was just an old-fashioned drunk. He was a skilled painter. He could paint, drunk off his ass, without any masking tape, as quick as can be. He also wore actual white painter's pants, which gave him a certain authority. In fact, it took me about two weeks to figure out what a raging drunk he really was. Now, I have a high tolerance for crazed behavior, but what constitutes an alcoholic in my book is someone who drinks a 12-pack of crappy warm beer in the middle of the day. During a lunch break one day, I walked past his van and witnessed this bizarre activity. I politely declined a warm Milwaukee's Best.

Peter, although he looked like he was a member of the Charlie Daniels Band, was really into alternative music. He listened to 770 Radio K (the station from the University of Minnesota) on a little boom box at the worksite. He started to come see my band play. Peter would usually get far too wasted, but in the context of a rock show, it just seemed it like another rowdy night.

"How do you like working in the rain?" the boss asked me one day. He wanted me to go out in the pouring rain and take apart a table. There are people who need to get things done and then there are people who like to make you do things because they can.

"I'll get to it later," I told him.

"Well, then you can get the hell out of here and not come back!"

"OK."

About a week later the clown called me, faked an apology, offered me a raise and told me he had a job in Minneapolis that he really needed me for. Still in need of cash, with no lucrative deals on the horizon, I grimaced and said yes. When I arrived at the location in Powderhorn Park, I realized why he bothered to call me. This place was really a dump. I believe "shit box" is the technical real estate term. While Mr. Jerk-Off was unlocking the door, Peter's van pulled up. At least I wasn't alone.

The house was filthy, smelly and hot. It had years of nicotine stains and God knows what else all over the walls. Peter and I were to scrub the walls with Tri Sodium Phosphate (TSP) and then paint them. It was, of course, about 80 or 90 degrees every day. And you could get mugged just walking down the street. Someone was always rifling through my Volvo in broad daylight.

So I scrubbed those miserable walls and dreamed of a greater tomorrow. This is what I went to graduate school for? I guess the answer was yes. Every week I got paid, bought my beer on the way home and played my guitar as much as possible. I made several weak attempts to get a teaching job. And then I played my guitar some more and scrubbed those walls. Eventually, I even painted them.

The job seemed endless and when I found myself drinking warm Milwaukee's Best in the middle of the day in Peter's van, I knew it was time to quite my little inner-city nightmare. So one Monday, I just didn't show up. The boss called and called. I ignored him. Sometimes total communication blackout is the greatest insult. I felt that Peter could just milk the job a little longer without me. One day I saw Peter the painter at the Big Top Liquor Store in the Midway buying more crappy beer. I was buying an expensive bottle of wine for a date. Class warfare?

A week later I saw him walking down University Avenue carrying a small box. I pulled over and told him to get in.

"What is in the box?"

"A goddamn water pump," he muttered and then went on a long diatribe about his Caravan. Peter lived in a bizarre storefront in Frogtown. I told him that Mopar invented the minivan. Peter wasn't impressed. In the driveway, sat the minivan. He knew what he was doing, but I was able to give him a hand pulling belts and handing him wrenches. We got that water pump installed. He thanked me for the ride and the help.

"Well," I said, "do you want to drive us to our next gig?"

And he did. He pulled up to the practice spot in the Caravan and we loaded in the amps, the guitars and the drums. I was pumped to play at the 7th Street Entry again! The drummer and I were also excited about not having to drive. There was a slight problem. It was 5:30 p.m. and our driver was already wasted. We decided to make the most of it, but when we got onto West I-94, I really started to freak out. I looked at the drummer and saw real fear in his eyes. I became a very aggressive copilot, being in the front-seat. I was screaming things like "Look OUT!" "Get into the next lane NOW! " Peter the painter just laughed, enjoying the fact that he was scaring the shit out of his us.

We finally made it to the little backdoor on 7th Street where you load in your gear. I never thought I would want to kiss the ground in Minneapolis, but came damn close that day. The gig was a blast. People go to the 7th Street Entry to ROCK and it is a great place to do it. I looked over at Peter a few times during the night—he looked really trashed. We arranged to get brought home by a friend who had a truck at the gig. I tried to get Peter to give me his keys, but he got really belligerent.

I saw Peter again at the Big Top about a week later. I wasn't buying fancy wine for a date, I was buying just slightly better beer than him. He told me that he had crashed the Caravan right by the post office that night in downtown Minneapolis. He fled the scene down to the river. He passed out under the bridge and then walked back to St. Paul the next morning. And that was that. The police never tracked him down. I am sure the Caravan was uninsured and most likely not even in Peter the painter's name. Peter now had a bicycle and I had once again cheated death on the roads and byways of the Seven County Metro Area.

1985 Ford E-150 (Record Deal)

On my many jaunts from the east coast back to the heartland, I had an occasion to stop and visit my older sister. She, her young son and husband were living in Lakeville, Ohio, an inner-ring suburb of Cleveland. I've driven straight through many times, but I will say, it is damn nice to stop and rest in a friendly abode.

My friend Mike and I had been in New York looking for a distribution deal for the *Poetry Grenade* record. We had barged into the office of Caroline Records and demanded that they listen to our LP. By some bizarre miracle, some grouchy New Yorker agreed to check it out. We sat on the couch in the waiting room whilst we heard the dude in his office drop the needle on each groove for just a moment, on the A side only. "I'll take 150 copies," he said gruffly, "at 3.25 a pop." Shocked, we stood up. Mike shook his hand and I ran out to the van to get the records while they cut a check. $487.50 was like a million dollars for us. And there was my name on that check: Paul D. Dickinson. But I knew that as residents of Minnesota, we were never going to be able to cash that check in New York.

We were sleeping on the hardwood floor of our friend Esther. We found this to be quite comfortable. NYC is perhaps the only place where lying down on a floor with no pillow or blanket seems reasonable. We felt like high rollers with the check tucked into my combat boot. All we really needed were limited funds for pizza, Budweiser tallboys, falafel sandwiches, and fuel back to St. Paul.

There is really no legal or safe place to park a car in New York. Also, my Minnesota plates glowed like a beacon parked on McDougal Street. That night we wanted to salute our completed mission. We celebrated in the tradition of our tribe: we went to a rock 'n' roll show. That night it was Dinosaur Jr. at CBGB's. Epic guitar mania, aloof girls, cans of beer downed from the deli across the street. I think my ears are still bleeding.

The next morning I rose early and went out to get coffee. The van: robbed. They smashed the "smoking" vent window. They took my CB radio, Mike's leather jacket and two boxes of our records. So we also received some "street distribution" for our LP. Seeing this as a sign to get the hell out of town, I woke up Mike, said goodbye to our hostess, and headed out. We felt a little shaky and violated, but we knew there was a safe place to sleep a mere 14 hours away.

When my sister opened the door she gave us a look that only a big sister could give, which, translated, meant: "You look like shit. What are you doing with your life?" But we were just so happy to be out of New York and off the road. The carpeted floor of the modest apartment seemed like the Taj Mahal. We immediately laid down and went to sleep.

I awoke in a daze several hours later, not quite sure where I was. Mike was still out cold. I always seem to sleep less anyone else. I sat there, staring into space. I then double-checked my duffel bag. I changed, putting on my last clean set of clothes. They looked a lot like the dirty set of clothes. Black Levi's jeans, a black Rolling Stones 1982 tour T-shirt. Clean socks and underwear, combat boots, size 8R. All of Devo has the same boot size, 8R. Here I was in Ohio, the birthplace of Devo, with my combat boots. I examined the check from Caroline Records. It was real. As a matter of pure instinct, I checked my wallet. We needed to cash that check.

My brother-in-law worked in a bank. While Mike slept like a baby, I found out where the bank was, drove into Cleveland and cashed the check. Now I had reversed that feeling I had been getting, the psychological distress I referred to as "low-cash-esteem."

I felt pretty good with my wad of cash. After filling the van with gas and buying two jugs of drinking water, I was ready to hit the road again. When I returned to the apartment in Lakeville, Mike was up from his nap and looked really out of it. Time had no meaning to us. My sister made us some sandwiches. Then she asked me for a favor. She and her family were moving back to Minnesota in a month, and she wanted us to haul some stuff in the van. It turned out that it was mainly my nephew's toys, sporting goods and various other cool things a kid would love. She boxed it up and we threw it in the truck. I asked for one final thing: a rubber band for my wad of cash. Now I was really ready to hit the road. It was getting dark, but I didn't care—I just wanted to finish this final leg of the journey. So we were merrily on our way. Soon we would be back in old St. Paul, back to my comfortable slacker life.

We were pumped. We had our little fun trip and we even had some $$. And then, out of nowhere, police lights were flashing. Oh shit. What? Us? Dear God. OK, OK, I pull over the van and we await our fate. This trooper turned out to be more like a storm trooper. He walked up to the van with his hands on this gun, which is never a good sign. "Keep your hands where I can see them! Why is your window broken? Did you steal this van?"

"No, sir. I have the registration to prove it." I was trying to be cooperative, but this hothead was scaring the shit out of me.

"Why didn't you fix it?"

"It happened in New York City. We just want to get home."

"Why were you in New York?"

"Ah… we are in a band." (Big mistake—but truly, I don't think I could properly explain to anyone why the hell I kept going to New York.) Well, the mere mention of a rock band really pushed this cop over the edge. He had us spread-eagle against the van. He gave us a spirited search and found my big wad of cash.

"What the hell is this?"

I had to admit, it looked like something a drug dealer might carry around. "Um… I just cashed a check. I have the stub to prove it." He put Mike in the back of the squad car. When they separate you that is a really bad sign. That means they want to interrogate you. He flipped me around and really got in my face.

"Are you transporting large quantities of cocaine, marijuana and heroin across state lines?"

"No, sir." Did he think he was going to trick me into saying yes?

"What the hell is in the boxes?"

"My nephew's toys."

"What? So I guess you don't mind if I search your van and your boxes of toys." He said the word "toys" with a certain disgust.

"No, sir." The frenetic search that followed was entertaining. He opened every box. He found G.I. Joe, he found Castle Grayskull, he even found the Fuzzy Pumper Barbershop, but he didn't find large quantities of narcotics. His dreams of a huge bust were dwindling. At least he didn't beat us; at least he didn't seize my cash. He begrudgingly got Mike out of the squad car and let us go. We crept east on I-90 locked in at 55 MPH, ready to get home and kiss the filthy blacktop of old St. Paul once again.

Toyota Celica

1982 Renault Alliance

I can't remember why Dolan gave me this car. It probably had a real problem that I fixed. Perhaps the car was dead when he left town. Sometimes it is crystal clear. I can remember every part in my filthy hand, every stripped bolt finally fitting into place. But other times it is a mechanical mishmash of fractured remembrance. Somehow I came up with the brilliant idea that I would drive this free car of dubious quality out to New York City, deliver it to Dolan, and fly black with a cheap one-way ticket. On the way, I was going to stop over in Vermont and go to the Old Boy's wedding. Vermont is just up the road from NYC, right?

The car looked good. It was a cool powder blue and it ran a lot better than the other Alliance I had. I put air in the tires, fueled up and left. I always drove right through Chicago, straight through the loop. It might be crowded as hell, or you might just fly right through on the Dan Ryan Expressway. I liked to get that full Chicago feel. I enjoyed seeing other bombed-out cars shooting sparks with dangling mufflers and bad suspensions. I felt an immediate alliance with those people. I never cut them off. Brand-new SUV? Get out of my way. The Renault and I made a pit stop at the Knute Rockne Rest Stop and "Oasis" in Indiana, where I actually examined the map for the first time. "Holy shit!" I said aloud at that picnic table, the map flapping in the breeze. This was when I realized that 1) Burlington, Vermont was a bit farther up north than I imagined, 2) Driving straight through Chicago was sort of a bonehead move, I could have taken a more efficient route via the Indiana tollway, and 3) How the hell was I going to get to Vermont without falling asleep at the wheel?

I really contemplated going to Northampton and bugging Zeke on Elizabeth Street, demand he drink beer with me and let me sleep on that famous couch. But then I thought better of it. According to the map, it was about 150 miles south of my new route, the route I actually planned with the help of Knute Rockne. My driving philosophy had always been "a minute not on the road is a minute not on the road," so I slammed my fountain drink and hit it.

I waited until I was in Ohio. Then I went to a real truck stop. A REAL truck stop has the following: 1) Showers, 2) Pornography, 3) A 24-hour café, and 4) White Cross (which the Chinese call Ma Huang). For this visit, I only wanted the 24-hour café, although the White Crosses were tempting. I overheard a trucker order his eggs, "extra greasy." Inspired, I ordered a trucker burger, which is a burger with an egg on top.

Pumped, full of dead cow and grease, I was ready for the cosmic blur of endless road. Damn, this is a big country. Isn't that the secret of America? If you don't like the town you are in, just go to another town. Rolling through almost every town in Ohio, Pennsylvania and New York, I thought, how did people end up here? I am damn certain that people drive through my town, St. Paul, and think, how the hell do people end up here?

Don't ask for details on how I got to Burlington, Vermont. Green signs, blue signs, state highway, tollway, thruway, county road, dead end, village centre. I found out where the wedding reception was located. The problem was I got there about eight hours before the event began. So I did what any red-blooded American would do, I slept in my car.

Fully rested, I found a McDonald's, went into the bathroom and got cleaned up in the sink. I purchased a cut of their cheap shit coffee, found a little park and changed into my suit. The Old Boy appeared to be marrying a 19-year old girl, but that was just my perception. He was teaching at a Catholic college up there in Vermont that seemed to specialize in lovely Quebecois maidens. Did he ask her in the third person? "The Old Boy would like to have your hand in marriage…" It was a fun wedding with plenty of food and drink, but I didn't imbibe—I thought I was going to drive to NYC after the wedding. Instead, I took the time to visit with the Old Boy's friends and family, although I cannot remember any of them except for the bride and the Quebecois bridesmaids.

After another night of sleeping in Club Renault, I was a little stiff. The locals at the wedding had told me it was a six-hour drive to NYC. There was a new development that concerned me, one that occurred in my final leg of my jaunt into Vermont. The damn front end started making a terrible racket—something I can only assume was related to the CV joint. At first I was afraid to inspect it. I know this sounds crazy, but sometimes looking at a car problem makes it worse. Upon a begrudging inspection, I saw a torn CV boot and looked away in disgust. Dear Lord, they can put a man on the moon, but they can't find a better way to make a front-wheel-drive front end?

What did it all mean? Would I fix it? Hell no. Would I perhaps die in a flaming wreck as the wheel collapsed on me while I was rolling along at highway speeds? Perhaps. I needed to adjust my route. What frightened me the most was driving on the Cross Bronx Expressway. The CBE is perhaps the last place on earth you would want any sort of part failure. I've seen the stripped wrecks strewn on the edge, some of them torched to a crisp. Those destroyed machines always spoke to me. They told me, "Beware, idiot who driveth crappy cars that fall apart and break down, cars you get for free or pay very little for… this, this could be you." As I crept through New England, the wounded front axle making its death moan, getting closer to New York City, I felt a sense of impending doom. So I rode down I-95 as long as I could stand it, feeling that death on the highway out in New England might be a bit more dignified than a roadside slaughter in New Jack City. I got off the highway somewhere in New York. It felt rural, but I could tell that NYC was near. I approached the city.

My ultimate mission was to deliver the Renault to a street in lower Harlem, right off of Broadway. So there I was, a backward Lewis and Clark, not searching for the edge of a continent or for awesome bodies of water, but for the beginning of the most famous street in the world. I went up and down strange hills. I got lost. I went to a crappy-looking gas station. Was I in Yonkers? I saw a very slick-looking black dude in a bronze Mercedes 300 SL. He looked busy, important. "Excuse me," I said. "Do you know where Broadway starts?"

"Oh yeah," he responded. He then launched into complicated directions at breakneck speed. I tried to follow along. He looked at my road-weary, hick-from-Hicksville white face with its stupefied expression. "Look, I'm going that way, follow me and I'll just point it out to you."

Via hill and dale, through what I imagined was Washington Irving's stomping grounds, I followed that Mercedes like there was no tomorrow. And this guy didn't drive slowly. I was just praying that this little French car, tailing a very solid German car, wouldn't just fall apart before I found the Great White Way. I was so in my head, concerned with my all-too-imminent destruction that I almost ran into the 300 SL when he came to a sudden stop. He stuck his arm out the window and pointed to the left. And then he just sped off before I could even thank him, and there I was, on Broadway.

The Renault and I crept down Broadway. I did feel like Rip Van Winkle. Unlike coming in on the CBE, I felt like I had come out of a mythical garden, awakened by all this activity and clamor. I was jacked. Crouching over and peering at the street numbers, I had a long way to go. But I did it; I eventually took that right turn on West 104th Street and delivered the car, trashed CV joint and all, to the door of Dolan. He was home. He lived in a very cool old row house with huge windows. We trudged up the stairs and sat at his kitchen table. I handed him the keys to the Renault and he handed me a Budweiser tallboy. It felt so damned good to be alive.

Chevy El Camino

Ford Econoline E-150

Somehow on our tour, we ended up in Louisville, Kentucky for a week. We gigged at Tewligans and then just stayed for a while. I met grown men who rode around on BMX bikes. I ate ribs. I may have pissed people off. I remember feeling like I was sliding backward down a huge mountain. It had nothing to do with Louisville. It was all my own never-ending struggle with reality. The drummer asked me, "Why are you in such a bad mood?" I had no answer. Let me tell you something: It is the days off that kill a band. If you have a show every night, then you have a mission, a damn reason to live, a girl to pick up, a free beer to receive, a T-shirt to sell.

Our next show was at Maxwell's in Hoboken, New Jersey. We made a rash decision to drive straight to New York City in order to arrive one day before the gig. It is quite a bit cheaper (if you don't go to Churchill Downs) to hang out in Louisville, but the siren call of New York is damn strong. The E-150 was holding up well with the abuse of the road. I did take care of Mr. E-150. Some people may give their cars a female name, but this van was my comrade, my brother in arms. With a van you can drive straight on through the night. Why stop at a crummy hotel? Just keep on driving.

Through the nightscape and early dawn we rode through a blur of states. We all took turns driving. Our planning and calculations were a bit off. We arrived in NYC on a Sunday morning at 9. None of the lowlife people we knew in New York would be awake for hours. We sat in the van in a daze in the East Village. We really didn't know what to do. We tried to sleep right there on the street, but even at that early hour on a Sunday, NYC is just too loud. So we just started driving around, wasting fuel.

And then a miracle happened. We crept down St. Mark's Place at around 10:30 a.m. and it looked like—yes, it was true—the door was propped. The Holiday Cocktail Lounge looked open. Some people call this a "dive" bar. Well, in Minnesota, we just call it a bar. My cousin had introduced me to this place for its cheap drinks and unique atmosphere. We locked up the van, hiding the amps and guitars under the custom bed. Some bands travel with a dog to protect their gear. I stumbled into the Holiday, sore from driving and sleeping on floors. The antique Ukrainian bartender was behind the bar, open for business. The thought of drinking another beer that morning made me ill. I eyed the booths in bad light in the back. I think the old guy actually remembered me.

"Hello, sir. You know, my friends and I have been drinking for days. And we plan to keep drinking. We just got into town from Kentucky. Do you think we could rest for a few hours in those booths in the back?" I waited for an answer as my band mates stared at me in disbelief.

"OK," he said with a gesture toward the back of the bar. And we slept, and slept. I slept like I was in a five-star hotel. I think I was out for about three hours. I awoke and there were a few barflies at the bar. Sunlight was peering through the open door. I walked up to the bar and glanced back at the booths. I saw my band mates slowly sitting up.

"I'll take three Budweisers."

"OK."

Later that day, after hanging out in that bar all day, we finally got into the loft in Brooklyn where we were crashing. It was a cool place with plenty of room. We decided to take another nap before the gig. I tried, but I was a little restless. As I lay there, staring at the high industrial ceiling, I swear I heard Spanish and the jangling of tools.

No, I thought, you are just being a paranoid kid from Minnesota. Relax, this is supposed to be a good neighborhood.

We all piled into the van, excited to go play the gig. I got in the truck, get comfortable in my custom captain's chair, and turn the key. Click. Click. Click. "What the fuck?" I run outside and open the hood. No battery. Paranoid indeed.

We caught a cab to Hoboken with all the guitars and a few cymbals. The other band was cool about us using their gear. In fact, I got to use a monster Marshall stack that made my guitar sound huge—much better than Marlboro (yes, the cigarette company) amp that I used. It was a rowdy crowd. We really were shredding through the set. Some kid untied the laces to my Converse high-tops. I hesitated for a minute, and then kicked him in the face. This was the right move because it made the crowd go wild. Later, that kid bought a CD.

The next day, I was poring over the Yellow Pages, not knowing where I was or how to get where I wanted to go. I just started calling auto parts stores I thought were in Williamsburg. I received directions from a guy to get a battery rated for the van. I am a cheap bastard, I'll be the first to admit it. And I've tried all sorts of weird used batteries transferred out of old cars, but it really makes sense to get the battery "rated" for your specific vehicle. The walk to the parts store wasn't too bad. The walk back to the loft, with a 47-pound battery, was really bad. I realized I looked like I had stolen the battery I had just purchased to replace the battery that was stolen. After stopping a few times to rest, I finally installed all 770 Cold Cranking Amps under the hood. The key was turned, the van fired up, and I was once again back in the game.

1985 Econoline Van (Riot Girls)

This van, this van, this van! I've lived and died in this van, loved and lost in this van, and now it was time to say goodbye to my dear old friend. And yes, Van, there were times I wanted to drive you off of a cliff, to set fire to you, to fire a 12-gauge straight at your crappy electrical system, but alas, I couldn't do it. And now it was time to send you, Mr. E-150, on another mission worthy of your legacy. Yes, indeed, I'm sending you off with the Riot Girls.

We had been going back and forth for a while. I didn't mind all the negotiating, because it was with a cute girl. If it was a dude, I would have told him to get lost a long time ago. I also liked the fact that she was going to drive my van out to Los Angeles with a bevy of other cute girls, rolling about on the custom bed. The van had 155,000 miles on it, but I was confident it would get them to California (but perhaps not back). Yet there comes a time when a man needs $800. If she had the cash, I'd just walk about to St. Paul. I drove over to the address. It was an extremely nice house in Kenwood. I only say "nice house" when I mean it. I think she thought I was being sarcastic.

It turns out that it was a good move. You really do need to make your presence know in the world of auto sales. I gave her a few pointers on the van. I showed her the infamous ignition modulator and the Cure and Black Flag tapes that come with the machine. I instructed her on how to set up the extremely cool bed in the back of the van. I think she was paying attention, I couldn't really tell.

Junker Dreams

She finally gave me my $800. I use her phone and call Mr. V. I told him to meet me at the Red Dragon bar. Being in Minneapolis, I got lost. And even though I drove there, I got a bit turned around on foot. I found Lyndale Avenue and I took my little walk toward that infamous watering hole. It is amazing how eight $100 bills can put you in a cheery mood. You just can't be too superstitious and live in the city. As I strolled past the CC Club, in the heart of what I always called the "Rock 'n' Roll Ghetto." I thought of past romances and grandiose dreams. Of so many plans that went up in flames. I pulled open the heavy door to the Red Dragon. The place was full of lowlife, daytime drinkers. It was all a living, breathing cautionary tale. I drank my Budweiser out of the bottle, tipped heavily and then stepped out into the glaring light. Mr. V rolled up in a Volvo wagon, I gave him a $100 bill and we went back to St. Paul.

Oh Van, Mr. Van—I checked up on you and I heard about your fitting demise. Those chicks did move themselves and all their barrettes, spiked belts, Converse high-tops, and cassette tapes out to California in your sturdy galley of Detroit Steel. They slept in your custom bed on the streets of Beverly Hills. They blasted around to Hollywood clubs, peering out of your curtained windows into the endless madness that has engulfed so many.

And then they took a trip to San Francisco. Your ailing Ford LTD junkyard transmission groaned and slipped up and down those hills. Your brake pads reduced to mere shadows, a screeching symphony of metal upon metal, barely stopping your hulking bulk and precious cargo. But you did it. You not only got them out to California, but around California.

But one night, while out in San Francisco, you were stolen. And the cops found you three days later in Oakland, torched to a crisp. Oh, Mr. Van, you were such a badass truck. I knew you were going to go out in a blaze of glory. You served so many for so damn long. *Adios, sayonara, goodbye.*

Volvo 240

1984 Volvo 240 DL Wagon

The vast Volvo conspiracy...1984 240 DL Wagon. Dear Reader, I found out the hard way that it is real dangerous to get a car that has been sitting around for a long time, especially in the great state of Minnesota where everything rusts at a hyper pace.

At first one thinks, wow, this car isn't being abused! It is just waiting for me to abuse it. Romantic visions of a car sitting in a farmer's filed awaiting your command. Well, I got this wagon out of a field in Forest Lake, Minnesota, and it truly almost led to my last mission ever. But with these beater cars, there is no ejection seat, not even the fate of being held in a bamboo cage by the enemy. No, sir, it is just all death, mutilation and perhaps a jail cell waiting at the roll of the dice. It was in this bucket that I proved my love to my beloved.

Now, diamond rings and trips to Mexico are nice, but I drove a $300 car 6.3 times from St. Paul to Chicago like a bat out of hell just to see her. I didn't open the hood, I didn't change the oil, I just put on my leather jacket and stomped on the gas. The speedometer was broken, so only the good Lord and the Wisconsin State Patrol knew my true sped. Of course, right before the seventh attempt, just when it got cold as hell, the starter went out on me.

The manic mechanic was doing a stint in the Carleton County jail up north. He was bored, so he called me. When people call you from jail it actually costs you money, they charge a fee to your phone. It is like you are being punished for knowing lowlife individuals. In fact, I have been punished by knowing this one, again and again, over and over. But I needed his counsel dearly.

"Call me back on my cell!" I cried. I bolted over to my brother's garage and cranked up the heat on the heater. I confess to you that I had to drink three beers just to crawl on my piece of cardboard underneath that hunk of Swedish steel. The power hippie had leant me a 19mm flex socket to turn the elusive bolt that holds the starter in place. This is the toughest part. Of course the bolt was rusted in its place, ice-cold and immovable. I soaked it in WD-40. I drank another beer and warmed my hands by the heater. My cell rang.

"Have you bench-tested the starter?" the manic mechanic asked. I looked over at the bullet-shaped starter that I had stripped off another Volvo years ago. It sat there in silence, looking back at me.

"No."

"You better find out right now," was the gruff response.

Now, in a real garage, I'm sure they have an advanced way to test electrical pars. In my world, all this meant was hooking up jumper cables to the part in question. Growing up in Minnesota, how many times have I used jumper cables? At this point, it is almost like breathing air itself. I always stare at the battery and repeat the words my father taught me as a teenager: "Black on Black, Red on Red." Some chicken shits like to ground out the negative black clamp on the engine block; I've found that leads to lame results. I hooked up the cable to the battery and then to the starter that has "1982" stamped on it. This particular starter looks like it came of a drowned Spanish Galleon, but I'll be damned if when the cables were put upon it, it didn't click and jump like a frisky little animal. Thus bench-tested, I finally got it in the car and it started like a charm. I returned the 19mm flex socket because bad tool karma is something no man can live with. I went to the gas station and filled up on fuel. These trips to Chicago also happened to, of course, be timed at the same time as a gasoline price spike and I was hurting. As I've stated before, I owe so much to my friends—and they owe a lot to me. This happens to be a very special gas station that I can really tell you about now because it is no longer there. On Snelling and eastbound I-94, I pulled into pump 7 and started filling up the tank on the 240 DL. I looked into the gas station window and see the Mexican Rocker Chick. She smiles a beautiful smile. My car, full of complimentary premium gasoline, is ready for the trip. I get the thumbs-up from her and drive off. God bless America.

And so I am on my way, as Jim Dandy from Black Oak, Arkansas would say, "with a lot of motor under my wheels." Well, a 4-cylinder engine with fuel injection and a tank of free premium fuel, anyway. I usually made it door-to-door from Selby Avenue to Malden Street in six hours and fifteen minutes. I swear I knew every tree, every building, every billboard on that stretch of I-94 and I-90. So there I was plugging away, making my usual progress, deep inside Wisconsin, when the rear end started making terrible noises. My usual tactic of cranking up my Iron Maiden tape on the stereo just wouldn't drown out the racket, so I exited the highway at the mega stop, purchased a mega fountain drink and investigated my undercarriage.

After an unscientific examination of the rusty unknown of my rear drive train, I determined everything was OK and I resumed my journey. I was on the freeway for about five minutes when my environment radically changed. There was a terrible screeching noise of metal upon roadway that was deafening. I saw arcs of sparks in my rearview mirror. Steering my machine became difficult, but I somehow pulled it over to the shoulder. I sat there in shock, trying to figure out what really happened, when I turned to my left and saw my own tire pass me on the highway. I bolted outside the vehicle and saw that my axle and my hub were in flames. To show you how mega those mega sodas are, I put out the entire blaze with my beverage. My first instinct, of course, was to find the tire and try to put it back on, except there was nothing to put it onto. It must be that tire detachment at 70 miles per hour is a little hard on moving parts, as my hub had been transformed into a molten metal mess. I hitched a ride to the next truck stop and called a towing service that was posted next to the payphone. The car was towed to a garage outside Mauston and left in a mud pit. The mechanics eyed me suspiciously as I gathered up all my tools, my cassette tapes and my two-ton jack out of the Volvo. I knew, deep in my heart, that I was never going to see that car again. Call me superstitious, but I think it's a good idea to walk away from a car in which you nearly died. I paid $80 for the tow and told the Mauston mechanics I'd be in touch. The tow truck driver offered to drive me back to the truck stop from whence I came. A better idea dawned on me. "How far south will you drive me for $50 cash?"

"I'll drive you to the Flying J Truckstop in Janesville," he responded.

I still had some juice in my Motorola "Candy Bar" cell phone. I rang my girlfriend and asked her if she'd pick me up at a truck stop two hours from Chicago. She was shocked and concerned, but agreed to hit the road.

The tow truck driver was a jolly fellow. He was a Gulf War vet and he was impressed with my knowledge of military aircraft. He brought me into the Flying J with grand style, introducing me to the head waitress at the café, securing me a place to stash my belongings. I drank bad coffee and stared into the darkness, awaiting my rescue. I never thought I'd be so happy to see that little Toyota Celica GT. I rode to Chicago in a daze of adrenaline, so thankful to be alive. The last thing I grabbed from under my visor was a picture of my woman. I loved that picture, but I didn't even need to look at it. I would drive a thousand beater cars a million desperate miles just to see her. The last time I was there, I just saw her visage in multiple different views. I nearly wept, looking at her in that Mexican restaurant. This was a real beauty that every man believes he is born to find.

Once in Chicago, I called the mechanics in Mauston, Wisconsin. They weren't very perceptive. These rubes thought that they had a rich guy from Minneapolis. I was told that it would cost $1,500 to fix the axle. I tried not to laugh. I knew I was never going back for that car, but I wanted to somehow keep my options open. I told them I would call them back. I never did. The amount of quality parts on that car, including a mint front grille and clip, were worth quite a bit. If they were any sort of mechanics at all, they could make a fortune off all the parts on that Volvo. Sometimes you have to be unsentimental—just leave them behind in Wisconsin mud pits and move on.

It was there, a narrow fugitive from death with $6 in my pocket and an engagement ring from ancient Ireland, that I asked the hottest of all St. Paul Irish girls to marry me. She said yes, and I didn't care about cars, roads, or anything at all. But I did need to get back home to my teaching gig at the art school.

So after a weekend of celebrating being alive and slowly having a life, I went to the Northwestern University computer lab with my debit card. I had $50 on it. I found a one-way ticket on the crummy ATA airlines for $48.55. I flew home clutching a doctor's bag full of tools from my destroyed Volvo. It was full of wrenches, hammers and even a hacksaw.

They took away my can of WD-40, but let me take the rest of my kit right on the plane. Before I boarded that miserable, packed flight, I had a $4 Corona beer in the lame, overpriced bar at the Midway Airport.

When I arrived at the Minneapolis/St. Paul Airport, I had $2 to my name and no car. I didn't even have a ride home from the airport. I walked outside to see about getting a bus, when I saw a bashed-up red Volvo 240 sedan creeping toward me. The driver looked like he had just escaped from some sort of punk rock work camp.

"Are you Paul D.?"

"Yep"

"Hey, ah, Mr V. told me to pick you up."

I was a little nervous, but the Volvo, and the fact that I really had no other option, helped put me at ease.

So we cruised out of the airport, out to highway 5 over the river, into St. Paul. We went up Fairview, took a right on Selby Avenue and pulled right in front of 1773. During our little ride, we had talked about Volvos and I described to him in detail my brush with death upon the highway.

"Well, dude," (his name turned out to be Fritz), "that did cost me some gas money." I reached in my pocket and gave him my two dollars. He wasn't impressed.

"It is, believe me, all I have." I opened the door and got out.

I was home. I was in love, I was broke and I had finally run out of junker cars, but I didn't care. My life had been spared and extended. It was a cold fall night, yet I wasn't quite ready to go inside. I walked up the front lawn a bit, laid down on the cold ground, stared at the sky, and started to breathe.

CPSIA information can be obtained
at www.ICGtesting.com
Printed in the USA
BVHW012207230619
551502BV00004B/10/P

9 781933 435534